The Founding Fathers

The Founding Fathers

THE MEN BEHIND THE NATION

John S. Bowman, *General Editor*

JG PRESS

Published by World Publications Group, Inc.
455 Somerset Avenue
North Dighton, MA 02764
www.wrldpub.net

ISBN 1-57215-436-5

Editor: Emily Zelner
Designers: Stephanie Stislow & Lynne Yeamans
Production Manager: Ellen Milionis

Printed and bound in China by SNP Leefung Printers Limited.

1 2 3 4 5   06 05 03 02

Publisher's Note
The publisher would like to acknowledge the contributions of Jim Kaplan, Brooks Robards, Brian Turner, Robert Ullian, and Joel Carino, who also wrote the captions. And thank you to Carol Inskip for indexing.

PAGE 1: *The signing of the Declaration of Independence after a painting by Charles Dumaresq. Many of the men who helped to found the United States refused to sign the Declaration, some feeling it was too drastic a move too soon.*

PAGE 2: *Thomas Jefferson reads a draft of the Declaration of Independence to Benjamin Franklin after a painting by Clyde O. Deland. When Jefferson expressed dismay at edits made by Congress, Franklin told him, "I have made a rule, whenever in my power, to avoid becoming the draughtsman of papers to be reviewed by a public body."*

Contents

The term "Founding Fathers"—enforced by its traditional capitalization—tends to evoke the image of a small circle of august, almost Olympian men, an elite group responsible for the fundamental documents and institutions of the United States, in particular the Declaration of Independence and the Constitution. True, sometimes the term is expanded to include all the signers of these two documents (although ironically, only one of the small circle traditionally named a Founding Father signed both—Benjamin Franklin), but even then the image is one of rather "elevated" individuals: men apart from the common course of events and passions. In recent years, a prominent historian published a book titled *Band of Brothers* that seemed to be signaling that these men were more approachable if not chummy, but again, the subjects turned out to be the traditional small circle.

In this conventional version of the founding of the nation, much credit is given to the early and most strongly committed of the Founding Fathers—a Samuel Adams, a Patrick Henry—the men who by their bold words and activities sparked the revolution. Then much credit is given to the men who led the colonists through the Revolutionary War—above all, George Washington in combat, Benjamin Franklin in diplomacy. And then credit is given to the men who created the seminal documents—Thomas Jefferson and James Madison in particular—and to those who held

LEFT: *A decorative engraving from 1860 depicting the signers of the Declaration of Independence emerging from Independence Hall in Philadelphia.*

View of The ATTACK on BUNKER'S HILL, with the Burning of CHARLES TOWN, June 17, 1775.

Drawn by. M.ʳ Millâr. · *Engraved by Lodge.*

ABOVE: A 1783 engraving of the Battle of Bunker Hill. Although British forces technically won the battle, their victory was a pyrrhic one, with losses far greater than those of the Americans. In order to reserve their ammunition, American commanders ordered, "Don't fire 'till you see the whites of their eyes!"

high posts in the nation's government in the first years—Alexander Hamilton, John Adams.

This book takes a different approach. It in no way denies the major roles played by these men, but it recognizes that there were far more men who played active roles in the founding of the United States of America. (And by the way, it must be recognized that women, no matter how influential in their husbands' lives—as for example, Abigail Adams—did not get a chance to play an active role in the founding.) This not only makes for a far more interesting and multilayered story, but it is the underlying thesis of this book that it is a version of events far truer to history. And it is a story that stretches over more years than is often accorded to the founding of the United States.

One omission in this extended family of Founding Fathers might seem to call for explanation. No one makes it into this group solely because of his military contributions or battlefield exploits. This is by no means intended to ignore or belittle the invaluable contributions of such men as Nathaniel Greene, Daniel Morgan, John Paul Jones, Francis Marion, Anthony Wayne, and George Rogers Clark. Clearly, they and the men they commanded in battles made it possible for the so-called Founding Fathers to conduct their affairs. But their story is a different one; a story of military achievements worthy of all the praise and honors

THE "MINUTE-MEN" OF THE REVOLUTION.

of the nation they did indeed help to found. Likewise, we mean no disrespect to the many men who played significant roles at critical moments in the early decades—men such as Alexander McDougall, the bold leader of the Sons of Liberty in New York City, or Paul Revere, who roused the Minutemen with his "midnight ride." This book, however, focuses on those who gave the greater part of their lives to creating a nation mainly through their words and government service.

Because the approach taken here opens up the image of the Founding Fathers—gets away from what has been called the "white marble bust" version of these individuals—readers may be in for some surprises. For one thing, many of these men turned out to be political opponents of one another. In some instances, their opposition went far beyond what is regarded as standard political disagreements; it became downright hostile and vicious (and in at least one case, literally murderous: Alexander Hamilton was killed in a duel with his arch rival, Aaron Burr). Another surprise may well be to discover how many of these men often resisted endorsing some of the crucial stages in the founding process:

George Washington: Letter to John Francis Mercer
September 9, 1786

Dear Sir,
Your favor of the 20th. ulto. did not reach me till about the first inst. It found me in a fever, from which I am now but sufficiently recovered to attend to business. I mention this to shew that I had it not in my power to give an answer to your propositions sooner.

With respect to the first. I never mean (unless some particular circumstances should compel me to it) to possess another slave by purchase; it being among my first wishes to see some plan adopted by [the Legislature by] which slavery in this Country maybe abolished by slow, sure, & imperceptable degrees....

I shall rely on your promise of Two hundred pounds in five weeks from the date of your letter. It will enable me to pay the workmen which have been employed abt. this house all the Spring & Summer, (some of whom are here still). But there are two debts which press hard upon me. One of which, if there is no other resource, I must sell land or negroes to discharge....

I am. D[ea]r Sir
Y[ou]r Most Obed[ien]t H[onora]ble Ser[vant]

Go: Washington

Many initially opposed breaking away from Britain; some refused to sign the Declaration of Independence; some refused to attend the major convocations or, after attending, refused to endorse the Constitution; some actually used their influence and eloquence to oppose adopting the Constitution; some resigned their high posts in the early presidential administrations; some retired to their private homes, embittered at the course the new nation was following.

How, then, can such men possibly qualify as Founding Fathers? Because this book interprets the foundation of the United States of America as resting on something other than a checklist of "proper positions taken." It has chosen to interpret the fundamental American spirit, its basic values and goals, in the broadest sense. What mattered was that these men felt free to take independent positions, to speak out, to differ, to disagree, to oppose. The American historian Henry Steele Commager put it as well as anyone: "If our democracy is to flourish, it must have criticism; if our government is to function, it must have dissent."

That was why the colonists were willing to break away from a monarchy, why they fought to establish a new nation. And then they trusted that the new nation would respect the opinions of a minority, even that of a lone voice. As Jefferson said

BELOW: *A 1775 British political cartoon in which George III and Lord Mansfield, the chief justice of the King's Bench, ride in a carriage pulled by the horses "Obstinacy" and "Pride" toward an abyss that is war with the American colonies.*

in his first inaugural address: "Though the will of the majority is in all cases to prevail, that will, to be rightful, must be reasonable." And when there was a move to clamp down on this minority, on disagreement, on outspoken opposition—as there was with the Alien and Sedition Acts of 1798—Americans again took to expressing their strong resistance, not through acts of violence but through their eloquent words and legislative votes.

Democracy, it has long been noted, can be "messy," and there should be no avoiding the fact that the words and actions of the Founding Fathers were often messy. And let us admit that there were in fact several incidents of violence. The Hamilton-Burr duel has been mentioned, but there would also be Shays's Rebellion in Massachusetts (1786–87) and the Whiskey Rebellion in Pennsylvania (1794). But as will emerge throughout this book, the Founding Fathers themselves usually fought a "war of words." That meant a steady barrage of pamphlets, books, letters, proposals, resolutions, legislation, judicial decisions, treaties, and the most important of these—along with several lesser known but no less revealing—are excerpted throughout this book. The sheer number of words that several of these men produced—all written out by hand—is quite astonishing (and, to be frank, sometimes mind-numbing in their sheer quantity). But better these words than bullets. That, too, was one of the legacies that the Founding Fathers tried to leave to the inheritors of the nation they founded.

There may be yet another surprise in this book's presentation of these Founding Fathers, and that is the fact that many of them held beliefs or advanced ideas that we today find unsettling or repugnant. The most obvious instance—and the one that has been long recognized and widely discussed as a major flaw in our nation's foundation—is the fact that a number of these

BELOW: *A 1794 engraving of the Whiskey Rebellion in Pennsylvania, showing a mob protesting federal liquor taxes by tarring and feathering a tax collector. It was the first test of the new federal government's power, and also the only time a sitting president personally led a military force in the field.*

FAMOUS WHISKEY INSURRECTION IN PENNSYLVANIA.

UNITED STATES SLAVE TRADE.
1830.

individuals not only defended slavery but actually owned slaves. Perhaps equally disturbing will be the discovery that some of these same men—Washington and Jefferson being perhaps the most prominent—privately expressed their abhorrence of the practice of slavery even while possessing slaves. Jefferson's discussion of African-Americans in his *Notes on the State of Virginia* (1785), in its mix of insights into the curse that slavery had placed on the United States and his incredibly "scientific" notions about the people themselves, is one of the most embarrassing documents of any of the Founding Fathers. The compromise—and like it or not, but compromise, too, has always been an essential element in the survival of the American nation—were the terms in the Constitution. On the one hand, the importation of slaves was outlawed after 1808, but on the other hand, slaveholding states were allowed to include three-fifths of the total number of slaves as part of the population on which was based their representation in Congress.

Some of the Founding Fathers held still other ideas that most Americans have long since rejected. There is no denying, for instance, that all these men were of white Anglo-Saxon Protestant stock and most were relatively prosperous property-owners. Several were highly distrustful of creating a pure democracy—of turning the government over to the "masses." The result were such constitutional terms as limiting the vote to men, imposing an electoral college to serve as a sort of brake on sheer majorities, and electing senators by state legislatures, not by a direct vote.

But it was these same men who created the means to amend the Constitution—who recognized that there would be a need to adapt to the evolution of old and the emergence of new values over time. And perhaps that might highlight the final point about why these men continue to deserve their special status in the eyes of Americans. As stated at the outset, it should not be because they were somehow beyond mere human beings—unapproachable paragons of pure virtue. Their words were not written in stone, their institutions were not cast in bronze. They were not deities. They were not immortals. They were Founding Fathers, with all the human limitations and imperfections such men have.

Thomas Jefferson:
Writing about African–Americans in
Notes on the State of Virginia
1785

It will probably be asked, Why not retain and incorporate the blacks into the state, and thus save the expense of supplying, by importation of white settlers, the vacancies they will leave? Deep rooted prejudices entertained by the whites; ten thousand recollections, by the blacks, of the injuries they have sustained; new provocations; the real distinctions which nature has made; and many other circumstances, will divide us into parties, and produce convulsions, which will probably never end but in the extermination of the one or the other race. To these objections, which are political, may be added others, which are physical and moral. The first difference which strikes us is that of colour. Whether the black of the negro resides in the reticular membrane between the skin and scarf-skin, or in the scarf-skin itself; whether it proceeds from the colour of the blood, the colour of the bile, or from that of some other secretion, the difference is fixed in nature, and is as real as if its seat and cause were better known to us. And is this difference of no importance? Is it not the foundation of a greater or less share of beauty in the two races? ...The circumstance of Superior beauty, is thought worthy attention in the propagation of our horses, dogs, and other domestic animals; why not in that of man? Besides those of colour, figure, and hair, there are other physical distinctions proving a difference of race. They have less hair on the face and body. They secrete less by the kidneys, and more by the glands of the skin, which gives them a very strong and disagreeable odour. This greater degree of transpiration renders them more tolerant of heat, and less so of cold than the whites.... They seem to require less sleep. A black after hard labour through the day, will be induced by the slightest amusements to sit up till midnight, or later, though knowing he must be out with the first dawn of the morning. They are at least as brave, and more adventuresome. But this may perhaps proceed from a want of fore-thought, which prevents their seeing a danger till it be present.... When present, they do not go through it with more coolness or steadiness than the whites. They are more ardent after their female: but love seems with them to be more an eager desire, than a tender delicate mixture of sentiment and sensation. Their griefs are transient.... In general, their existence appears to participate more of sensation than reflection....

Comparing them by their faculties of memory, reason, and imagination, it appears to me that in memory they are equal to the whites; in reason much inferior, as I think one could scarcely be found capable of tracing and comprehending the investigations of Euclid; and that in imagination they are dull, tasteless, and anomalous...They astonish you with strokes of the most sublime oratory; such as prove their reason and sentiment strong, their imagination glowing and elevated. But never yet could I find that a black had uttered a thought above the level of plain narration; never saw even an elementary trait of painting or sculpture. In music they are more generally gifted than the whites with accurate ears for tune and time, and they have been found capable of imagining a small catch. Whether they will be equal to the composition of a more extensive run of melody, or of complicated harmony, is yet to be proved.....

Whether further observation will or will not verify the conjecture, that nature has been less bountiful to them in the endowments of the head, I believe that in those of the heart she will be found to have done them justice. That disposition to theft with which they have been branded, must be ascribed to their situation, and not to any depravity of the moral sense. The man, in whose favour no laws of property exist, probably feels himself less bound to respect those made in favour of others... And whether the slave may not as justifiably take a little from one, who has taken all from him, as he may slay one who would slay him? That a change in the relations in which a man is placed should change his ideas of moral right or wrong, is neither new, nor peculiar to the colour of the blacks....

There must doubtless be an unhappy influence on the manners of our people produced by the existence of slavery among us. The whole commerce between master and slave is a perpetual exercise of the most boisterous passions, the most unremitting despotism on the one part, and degrading submissions on the other.... The man must be a prodigy who can retain his manners and morals undepraved by such circumstances. And with what execration should the statesman be loaded, who, permitting one half the citizens thus to trample on the rights of the other, transforms those into despots, and these into enemies, destroys the morals of the one part, and the amor patriae of the other.... With the morals of the people, their industry also is destroyed. For in a warm climate, no man will labour for himself who can make another labour for him. This is so true, that of the proprietors of slaves a very small proportion indeed are ever seen to labour. And can the liberties of a nation be thought secure when we have removed their only firm basis, a conviction in the minds of the people that these liberties are of the gift of God? That they are not to be violated but with his wrath? Indeed I tremble for my country when I reflect that God is just: that his justice cannot sleep for ever: that considering numbers, nature and natural means only, a revolution of the wheel of fortune, an exchange of situation is among possible events: that it may become probable by supernatural interference! The almighty has no attribute which can take side with us in such a contest. But it is impossible to be temperate and to pursue this subject through the various considerations of policy, of morals, of history natural and civil. We must be contented to hope they will force their way into every one's mind. I think a change already perceptible, since the origin of the present revolution. The spirit of the master is abating, that of the slave rising from the dust, his condition mollifying, the way I hope preparing, under the auspices of heaven, for a total emancipation, and that this is disposed, in the order of events, to be with the consent of the masters, rather than by their extirpation....

Part One
Igniting a Revolution
(1763–1775)

There was a time when the American Revolution was treated and taught as though it began 1775. The Battle of Lexington and Concord, the capture of Fort Ticonderoga, the Battle of Bunker Hill, the defeat of Lord Dunmore at Great Bridge, the capture of the *Margaretta* in Maine—these stirring events were regarded as launching the Revolution. But for some time now, the American Revolution has been placed in a much broader historical framework, and not only are its origins incorporated into the story of this revolution, the Revolutionary War itself is now regarded as a part of the history of the founding of the nation. As a result, some of the major players in these pre-hostilities years are recognized as worthy of consideration as among the Founding Fathers.

It is generally agreed that 1763 is the legitimate "seed" year for what would blossom into the revolution. For it was in 1763 that not only did Britain sign the Treaty of Paris that ended the Seven Years War and left Britain in control of much of North America, it also was the year that King George III issued the proclamation that forbade all Europeans to move west of the Appalachians. It was also the year that Britain announced it was going to maintain a standing army in the colonies—ostensibly to defend British North America from the French and Spanish, but clearly it was going to be able to keep an eye on the colonists.

PREVIOUS PAGE: The Battle at Bunker's Hill, *painted by John Trumbull, who in a 1789 letter to Thomas Jefferson wrote, "The greatest motive I had or have for engaging in or for continuing my pursuit of painting has been the wish of commemorating the great events of our country's Revolution."*

BELOW: *An engraving by Paul Revere depicting British warships landing in Boston Harbor in 1768.*

The Great Financier, or Britiſh Œconomy for the Years 1763. 1764. 1765.

ABOVE: *An illustration from the Boston Gazette newspaper on March 12, 1770, showing coffins bearing the initials of those killed at the Boston Massacre: Samuel Gray, Samuel Maverick, James Caldwell, and Crispus Attucks.*

RIGHT: *A British political cartoon from 1765 depicting British Prime Minister George Grenville holding a scale, representing the British economy, labeled "Savings" and "Debt." A Native American, representing the colonies and wearing a yoke labeled "Taxed without Representation," waits to add his savings to the scale.*

Even before 1763, of course, some prominent colonists were becoming increasingly more outspoken in their opposition to certain actions by Britain's Parliament. Among the most eloquent of these was James Otis in Massachusetts, who was speaking out and writing in opposition. But it was the passage of various acts, most of them imposing taxes or financial obligations of one kind or another—the Sugar, or Revenue, Act (1764), the Quartering Act (1765), the Stamp Act (1765) and the Townshend Acts (1767)—that truly roused the opposition by such men as Patrick Henry, Samuel Adams, Richard Henry Lee, and George Wythe. Whether as members of their respective states' legislatures or as private citizens, they spoke and wrote with increasing vehemence against what they perceived as unlawful demands, taxes, and actions by the British. In February 1766, for example, prominent men of Westmoreland County, Virginia, led by Richard Henry Lee, adopted what are known as the Westmoreland Resolves, a bold attack on the Stamp Act's requirements. And in 1768, Samuel Adams took the lead by composing a letter that circulated among the colonies' assemblies and called on them to join Massachusetts in resisting the taxes and other expenses imposed by Parliament. And when on March 7, 1770, British soldiers in Boston fired on a group of protesters they saw as threatening violence, Samuel Adams was among those who promoted this as the Boston Massacre.

It was after this episode, too, that Samuel Adams and Richard Henry Lee took the lead in encouraging the colonies to form what are generally known as Committees of Correspondence—basically to keep communities throughout the colonies informed of their rights and to give them a sense of unity in resistance. But it should be said that not all the Founding Fathers were ready to take up radical positions at this time. Benjamin Franklin, for one, was in London effectively as the ambassador for the colonies, and although he had defended the actions of the colonies before the House of Commons in 1766, he tried his best to work for a peaceful reconciliation between them and Britain. Meanwhile, John Adams, as a professional lawyer, set aside his personal beliefs and defended the British soldiers in their trial for the Boston Massacre.

Then in 1773, Parliament passed the Tea Act, which imposed a tax on tea that the colonists would have to pay for their favorite beverage. This so aroused the colonists that in several ports—Philadelphia, Annapolis, and Charles Town—the colonists took various actions to demonstrate their opposition to this tax. But it was in Boston that the most dramatic incident took place: On December 16, 1773, a group of Boston "patriots" disguised as Indians boarded three British ships carrying tea and threw 167 tea

The Preamble to the Suffolk Resolves
1774

At a meeting of the delegates of every town & district in the county of Suffolk, on Tuesday the 6th of Septr ., at the house of Mr. Richard Woodward, of Deadham, & by adjournment, at the house of Mr. [Daniel] Vose, of Milton, on Friday the 9th instant,... a committee was chosen to bring in a report to the convention, and the following being several times read, and put paragraph by paragraph, was unanimously voted, viz.

Whereas the power but not the justice, the vengeance but not the wisdom of Great-Britain, which of old persecuted, scourged, and exiled our fugitive parents from their native shores, now pursues us, their guiltless children, with unrelenting severity: And whereas, this, then savage and uncultivated desert, was purchased by the toil and treasure, or acquired by the blood and valor of those our venerable progenitors; to us they bequeathed the dearbought inheritance, to our care and protection they consigned it, and the most sacred obligations are upon us to transmit the glorious purchase, unfettered by power, unclogged with shackles, to our innocent and beloved offspring.... If a boundless extent of continent, swarming with millions, will tamely submit to live, move and have their being at the arbitrary will of a licentious minister, they basely yield to voluntary slavery, and future generations shall load their memories with incessant execrations. —On the other hand, if we arrest the hand which would ransack our pockets, if we disarm the parricide which points the dagger to our bosoms, if we nobly defeat that fatal edict which proclaims a power to frame laws for us in all cases whatsoever, thereby entailing the endless and numberless curses of slavery upon us, our heirs and their heirs forever; if we successfully resist that unparalleled usurpation of unconstitutional power, whereby our capital is robbed of the means of life;...whereby the charter of the colony, that sacred barrier against the encroachments of tyranny, is mutilated and, in effect, annihilated;...posterity will acknowledge that virtue which preserved them free and happy;.... —Therefore, we have resolved, and do resolve,...

There follows a list of nineteen resolves.

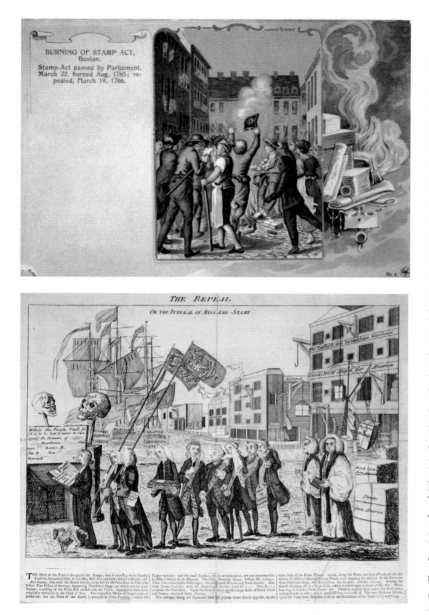

THE REPEAL

OR THE FUNERAL OF MISS AME-STAMP

ABOVE: A British cartoon from 1766 depicting a funeral procession for the Stamp Act. Prime Minister George Grenville bears a small casket with the inscription "Miss Ame— Stamp B. 1765 died 1766."

chests overboard—what quickly became known as the Boston Tea Party.

In retaliation for these various actions against the importation of tea, Parliament in 1774 passed what became known as the Intolerable, or Coercive Acts. These were aimed particularly at Boston—imposing stricter military control over the city, demanding payment for the destroyed tea—but also required all American colonists to pay for the housing and feeding of British troops. When some Bostonians rioted, the British military governor told his government in London that Massachusetts was virtually in a state of revolt. Now even Benjamin Franklin began to lose patience with the British. When the British governor of the colony of Virginia abolished its assembly—for calling for a day of prayer in support of Boston—Patrick Henry took the lead at a protest meeting of prominent Virginian colonists at the Raleigh Tavern in Williamsburg. And in Massachusetts, men from Boston and other Suffolk County towns drew up a series of indictments and protests that were known as the Suffolk Resolves; these virtually anticipated the Declaration of Independence of two years later.

The result of this growing resentment and resistance was that men from several colonies agreed to send delegates to what would become known as the First Continental Congress. Fifty-six delegates from twelve colonies (Georgia did not send any but agreed to support any decisions) gathered in Philadelphia between September 5 and October 26, 1774—among them were Samuel Adams, Patrick Henry, and Richard Henry Lee. Paul Revere also arrived bearing the Suffolk Resolves, the quite radical demands by a group of Massachusetts citizens, to be put before the Congress for its endorsement.

The delegates began by declaring that various acts passed by Parliament since 1763 were violating their rights. They then voted to stop importing goods from England or Ireland after December 1, 1774; if their concerns had not been satisfied by September 10, 1775, they agreed to stop exporting any goods to Britain or their possessions in the West Indies. The

Declaration of Rights they adopted on October 14 did not in any way call for independence, not even for representation in Parliament; most of the delegates were prosperous middleclass citizens and had no desire to break their ties with the motherland. But there was no avoiding the fact that some of the delegates were calling for far more radical positions. Indeed, by adopting the Suffolk Resolves, the Congress did come close to calling for independence.

The delegates left Philadelphia after agreeing to meet there again in May 1775 if they felt that it was necessary. And events would soon transpire that were beyond any of all but the most radical colonists' imaginings, let alone hopes. On February 9, 1775, Parliament declared Massachusetts to be in a state a rebellion. On April 19, 1775, British troops, after marching on Lexington and Concord to take control of British ammunition stores, fought the famous pitched battles. Thus, when the delegates assembled in Philadelphia for the Second Continental Congress on May 10, they realized that the colonies were effectively in a

WASHINGTON, APPOINTED COMMANDER IN CHIEF.

The Continental Congress, June 15th 1775, elected George Washington, Commander in Chief of all the forces raised, or to be raised, for the defence of the Colonies. He being then 43 years of age, and a member of that body, when President Hancock announced to Washington his appointment, he modestly and with great dignity signified his acceptance of the important trust.

revolution. They appointed George Washington commander in chief of the Continental army, but before he could take command in Cambridge, there was another battle in Boston, this one at Bunker (actually Breed's) Hill on June 17. On July 8, the Congress adopted a declaration on their reasons for taking up arms and in one last desperate effort, on July 10 they sent out a final appeal to King George III to seek some solution short of war.

But it was too late for statesmanship to save imperial Britain's colonies in North America. Few of the men present at this Congress in 1775 intended to engage in a revolution. But those who had taken the lead in bringing the American colonies to this stage would hereafter become known as Founding Fathers of a new nation.

RIGHT: *"The Bostonians in Distress," a political cartoon from 1774, symbolizing the blockade that followed the Boston Tea Party. Though a British cartoon, its meaning can be read either favorable or unfavorable to the colonists. Caged Bostonians hang from the Liberty Tree and are fed fish in exchange for a bundle labeled "Promises."*

James Otis

1725–1783

By general consensus, the buildup to the American Revolution occurred from 1763 to 1774. Since James Otis made a significant contribution as early as 1761, he might be described as our first Founding Father.

Like many patriots, Otis began as a conservative and loyalist. Born in West Constable on Cape Cod, Massachusetts, he graduated from Harvard in 1743 after complaining of its "miserable, despicable, and arbitrary government." Otis studied law with noted attorney Jeremiah Gridley and married heiress Ruth Cunningham. He practiced law in Plymouth and then in Boston, where his father James Otis, Sr.'s connections landed him positions first as justice of the peace in 1756 and later as deputy advocate general in the vice admiralty court in 1757. The younger Otis was talented, intelligent and industrious. He published *The Rudiments of Latin Prosody* (1756) and wrote an unpublished book on Greek prosody while earning a solid reputation as a lawyer.

Two events changed his outlook and life forever. In 1761, Sir Francis Bernard, the new governor of Massachusetts, passed over Otis, Sr., and chose Thomas Hutchinson as chief justice of the Superior Court. Young Otis claimed Hutchinson had promised to support his father. Hutchinson said he never sought the post and accepted it only when the governor refused to support Otis, Sr. A line in the sand was drawn between two influential families.

The same year, Customs Commissioner Charles Paxton began using the Writs of Assistance to stop illegal trade. These general search warrants authorized officials or their representatives to search businesses or homes for contraband without specifying the nature of the goods or their exact location.

Whether fueled by personal anger or professional outrage or both, Otis resigned as advocate general and agreed to represent the merchants opposing the Writs of Assistance. He refused any compensation saying, "In such a cause, I despise all fees." During a five-hour speech to the Superior Court on February 24, 1761, Otis argued that the writs violated the natural rights of colonists and that acts of Parliament nullifying these rights must be void. His language is as moving and powerful now as it was then:

> Now, one of the most essential branches of English liberty is the freedom of one's house. A man's house is his castle; and whilst he is quiet, he is as well guarded as a prince in his castle. This writ, if it should be declared legal, would totally annihilate this privilege. Custom-house officers may enter our houses when they please; we are commanded to permit their entry. Their menial servants may enter, may break locks, bars and everything in their way; and whether they break through malice or revenge, no man, no court can inquire. Bare suspicion without oath is sufficient.

Usually overlooked now is that Otis also called for something that was well ahead of most colonists' thinking—the liberation of all slaves: "The colonists [of Massachusetts] are by the law of nature free born, as indeed all men are white and black....Does it follow that it is right to enslave a man because he is black?"

A young lawyer named John Adams witnessed the speech and later declared, "Otis was a flame of fire!...He hurried away everything before him. American independence was then and there born; the seeds of patriots and heroes were then and there sown."

Otis did not win his case (which was decided ambiguously in 1766), but initiated a movement that would eventually culminate in the Fourth Amendment to the Constitution. In the wake of his *cause célèbre*, few officials

BELOW: *An obelisk designed by Paul Revere to mark the repeal of the Stamp Act in 1766. Otis protested the act as a violation of human rights. The obelisk was to be placed under the Liberty Tree in Boston, but the wood and paper monument burned down before it could be installed.*

dared to employ the writs. And Otis was just gathering steam. Two months after his speech, he was elected to the General Court (House of Representatives) amid a series of electoral rebukes to Bernard and Hutchinson. In 1762 he published his first political work, *A Vindication of the Conduct of the House of Representatives*, in which he compared the colonial governor's unauthorized expenditure of seventy-two pounds during a house recess to the king of England, who "could not spend a shilling the Commons had not appropriated."

Parliament began levying a series of taxes on the colonies that came to be known as the Grenville Acts, after Britain's Chancellor of the Exchequer. Protesting them at a Boston town meeting on May 24, 1764, Otis introduced the concept of no taxation without representation. His exact words, "Taxation without representation is tyranny," evolved into the popular "No taxation without representation." At the same meeting, Otis proposed that the colonies unite in opposition to Parliament.

Otis published his views on taxation in *The Rights of the British Colonies Asserted and Proved* (1764), warning of an impending "disenfranchisement of every civil right," and was named leader of the colony's Committee of Correspondence. In 1765, he went further in *A Vindication of the British Colonies* by ridiculing the idea of "virtual representation" by Parliament. Otis helped organize New York City's Stamp Act Congress, got the Massachusetts legislature to approve its goals, and recommended measures used by the Congress.

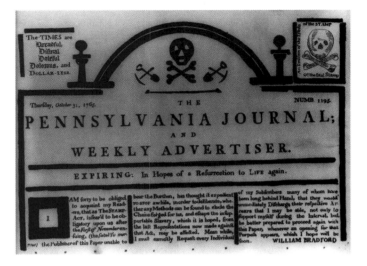

ABOVE: *The October 31, 1765, issue of the* Pennsylvania Journal and Weekly Advertiser, *with tombstone masthead, in which the publisher, William Bradford, announces the suspension of publication due to the Stamp Act, which went into effect on November 1.*

The Rights of the British Colonies Asserted and Proved
1764

Let no Man think I am about to commence advocate for despotism, because I affirm that government is founded on the necessity of our natures; and that an original supreme Sovereign, absolute, and uncontroulable, earthly power must exist in and preside over every society; from whose final decisions there can be no appeal but directly to Heaven. It is therefore originally and ultimately in the people. I say supreme absolute power is originally and ultimately in the people; and they never did in fact freely, nor can they rightfully make an absolute, unlimited renunciation of this divine right.... Tyranny of all kinds is to be abhor'd, whether it be in the hands of one, or of the few, or of the many.—And tho' "in the last age a generation of men sprung up that would flatter Princes with an opinion that they have a divine right to absolute power"; yet "slavery is so vile and miserable an estate of man, and so directly opposite to the generous temper and courage of our nation, that 'tis hard to be conceived that an englishman, much less a gentleman, should plead for it."...

Nonetheless, some Boston radicals considered Otis "a reprobate, an apostate and a traitor." In *A Vindication of the British Colonies*, he warned against bloodshed and independence, which would reduce the colonies to "a mere shambles of blood and confusion." At the Stamp Act Congress in 1765, and again when British redcoats landed in Boston in 1768, he argued for vehemence over violence. His opposition to Bernard and Hutchinson softened when his father was appointed chief justice and probate judge at Barnstable County's Court of Common Pleas (1763–65). Natural rights and social order warred for young Otis's loyalty, as did patronage politics and meritocracy. In the end, he redeemed his patriotic reputation by supporting the Stamp Act Congress's protest that the act violated fundamental human rights.

Otis was elected speaker of the Massachusetts House of Representatives but was vetoed by Governor Bernard in 1767. Undeterred, he and Samuel Adams circulated a letter urging other colonies to refuse new taxes. The Townshend Acts, Otis said, could drive colonists to revolt.

Among insurgents, he was probably the most visible and effective patriot in New England, if not America. Otis's contributions to liberty include a seminal concept of privacy. His views on taxation evolved into the rallying cry of the pre-revolution reformers. And he helped colonists everywhere unite. If Otis neither recommended violence nor suggested a break with the mother country, no other colonist did either during the 1760s.

Alas, all too suddenly, Otis's world collapsed. Outraged at statements Otis made in a 1769 newspaper article, a customs commissioner struck him on the head. Otis was severely injured and spiraled into bouts of insanity. He charged into the Battle of Bunker Hill without getting injured and wandered the streets of Boston, taunted by people who had admired him. His only son died in a British jail in 1777. His wife and one of two daughters were loyalists. A lightning bolt killed fifty-eight-year-old James Otis in May of 1783—the year the treaty was signed, ending the War for Independence.

Nonetheless Otis had thrown enough rhetorical bolts that struck and enlightened patriots like John Adams, John Hancock, Josiah Quincy and Paul Revere. Even the loyalist Hutchinson said he "never knew fairer or more noble conduct in a pleader, than in Otis," who "defended his causes solely on their broad and substantial foundations."

BELOW: *British Prime Minister William Pitt drives America, represented as a Native American in the carriage, toward an abyss. The horses represent members of Pitt's cabinet, one of which, Crafty, stands for Charles Townshend, who levied taxes that Otis felt could drive colonists to revolt.*

Richard Henry Lee

1733–1794

Richard Henry Lee, born in Westmoreland County, into a politically powerful Virginia family, played a major role in that state's political activities leading up to the Revolution. Had his wife's illness not kept him away from the Second Continental Congress at the crucial time, Lee might have penned the Declaration of Independence instead of Thomas Jefferson. As an Anti-Federalist Founding Father, Lee offered a deeply loyal, if dissident, voice during formation of the U.S. government. He was critical in particular of the absence of a bill of rights in the Constitution, a term limit for the office of president, and what he felt was an inadequate number of seats in the House of Representatives.

Educated at a private school in Wakefield, England, Lee married Anne Aylett in 1757, settling near Stratford Hall, which had been built by his father Thomas Lee, a founder of the Ohio Company (and which later became the home of Confederate General Robert E. Lee). After his first wife's death in 1768, Lee married Anne Gaskins Pinckard. Lee joined his father as a land developer in the Ohio Company and, later, the Mississippi Company. Beginning an active role in Virginia politics in 1758, Lee represented Westmoreland County in the Virginia House of Burgesses, where his forceful positions in favor of independence and against the slave trade cast him into the radical wing.

During the Stamp Act controversy, Lee first sought to become collector for the British, but he regained his standing with the Virginian patriots by taking the lead in composing the so-called Westmoreland Resolves in 1766, which went beyond protesting the act and actually proposed armed resistance against the British. He did not participate in the fight against the Townshend Acts because of a hunting accident in which he lost several fingers. By 1769, though, he joined the Virginia committee supporting the Massachusetts protest against those acts. As a result, Virginia governor Norborne Berkeley, Lord Botetourt, dissolved the assembly. In retaliation, the burgesses, including Lee, met in the Raleigh Tavern in Williamsburg to organize a boycott of British imports until the British repealed the Townshend Acts.

An important part of Lee's contributions leading up to the Declaration of Independence developed through his friendship with Samuel Adams, which led him to propose the formation of Committees of Correspondence for each colony in 1773. These committees circulated information about the Boston Tea Party and the pro-colonists climate

OPPOSITE: *A portrait of Richard Henry Lee, by Charles Willson Peale, painted on the occasion of Lee's election as president of the Continental Congress in 1784.*

in Great Britain, as reported by two of Lee's London-based brothers. Once the British closed Boston's port in response to the Boston Tea Party in 1774, Lee stood in the forefront of Virginia burgesses who called for a day of public fasting in support of the Massachusetts colonists. He also lobbied to close the Virginia courts and stop collection of British debts, before it was accomplished by Governor John Murray, Earl of Dunmore, when he dissolved the assembly. In response, the burgesses removed once more to the Raleigh Tavern to renew their support for the sanction against British imports.

The *TEA-TAX-TEMPEST*, or *OLD TIME* with his *MAGICK-LANTHERN*.

Lee's proposals to establish a colony-wide congress and a general sanction against exports to Great Britain led to the first Virginia Convention in August 1774. One of seven Virginians appointed to the First Continental Congress held in Philadelphia that fall, Lee gained recognition for his speaking skills, which rivaled Patrick Henry's and were reinforced by waves of his maimed hand covered with a black silk scarf. He played an important role at the Continental Congress by helping produce a colonists' declaration of rights; by supporting formation of a colony-wide boycott group; and by backing approval of Massachusetts's Suffolk Resolves, which opposed the British Coercive Acts.

In 1775, Lee continued to play an active role in the move toward independence. He favored the opening of American ports to foreign merchants, and his discussions with John Adams about setting up independent state governments led him to have Adams's views on the subject published in Virginia. At the Continental Congress in June 1776, it was Lee who introduced resolutions for independence, establishment of diplomatic relations with other countries, and a start to development of a confederation of colonies. His words. there led ultimately to the Declaration of Independence that: "These United Colonies are, and of right ought to be, free and independent States, that they are absolved from all allegiance from the British Crown, and that all political connection between America and the State of Great Britain is, and ought to be, totally dissolved."

Lee served a three-year term in Congress (1776–1779), where he helped appoint George Washington commander in chief. He returned to the Virginia legislature, where his reservations about the colonies' new union developed into a strong Anti-Federalist viewpoint. Lee returned to the Continental Congress (1784–1787) and became its president. During this period, he favored Jefferson's Ordinance of 1785 and helped draft the Northwest Ordinance. Poor health kept him from the 1787 Philadelphia

ABOVE: *A pro-colonist British cartoon, depicting Father Time giving a magical glass lantern presentation illuminating the clashes leading up to the Revolution. Two of Lee's brothers, based in London, helped report pro-colonist sentiment back to America.*

Westmoreland (Leedstown) Resolves
February 27, 1766

Roused by danger and alarmed at attempts, foreign and domestic, to reduce the people of this country to a state of abject and detestable slavery by destroying that free and happy condition of government under which they have hitherto lived.

We, who subscribe this paper, have associated and do bind ourselves to each other, to God, and to our country, by the firmest ties that religion and virtue can frame, most sacredly and punctually to stand by and with our lives and fortunes, to support, maintain, and defend each other in the observance and execution of these following articles —

FIRST: We declare all due allegiance and obedience to our lawful Sovereign, George the Third, King of Great Britain. And we determine to the utmost of our power to preserve the laws, the peace and good order of this Colony, as far as is consistent with the preservation of our Constitutional rights and liberty,

SECONDLY: As we know it to be the Birthright privilege of every British subject (and of the people of Virginia as being such) founded on Reason, Law, and Compact; that he cannot be legally tried, but by his peers; that he cannot be taxed, but by consent of a Parliament, in which he is represented by persons chosen by the people, and who themselves pay a part of the tax they impose on others. If, therefore, any person or persons shall attempt, by any action, or proceeding, to deprive this Colony of these fundamental rights, we will immediately regard him or them, as the most dangerous enemy of the community;

and we will go to any extremity, not only to prevent the success of such attempts, but to stigmatize and punish the offender.

THIRDLY: As the Stamp Act does absolutely direct the property of the people to be taken from them without their consent expressed by their representatives and as in many cases it deprives the British American Subject of his right to trial by jury; we do determine, at every hazard, and paying no regard to danger or to death, we will exert every faculty, to prevent the execution of the said Stamp Act in any instance whatsoever within this Colony. And every abandoned wretch, who shall be so lost to virtue and public good, as wickedly to contribute to the introduction or fixture of the Stamp Act in this Colony, by using stampt paper, or by any other means, we will, with the utmost expedition, convince all such profligates that immediate danger and disgrace shall attend their prostitute purposes....

SIXTHLY: If any attempt shall be made on the liberty or property of any associator for any action or thing to be done in consequence of this agreement, we do most solemnly bind ourselves by the sacred engagements above entered into, at the risk of our lives and fortunes, to restore such associate to his liberty and to protect him in the enjoyment of his property.

In testimony of the good faith with which we resolve to execute this association we have this 27th day of February 1766 in Virginia, put our hands and seals hereto.

Convention, but his Anti-Federalist *Letters from the Federal Farmer to the Republican* (1787–1788) circulated his views widely. Although he opposed the Constitution as anti-states rights and lacking a bill of rights, he went along with it once adopted. Elected to Congress in 1788 on a bill of rights platform, he led the move to adopt the first ten amendments. A strong-voiced patriot to the end, Lee found the Bill of Rights that was finally passed inadequate, because it could not stop the "tendency to consolidated Empire."

Samuel Adams

1722–1803

Born in prosperity, cast into poverty, Samuel Adams felt the sting of British interference in the conduct of Boston businesses, one of which, a brewery, was owned by his father. Adams's devotion to liberty was formed early, and after a period in the political wilderness he rose to become a leader, first in Massachusetts, then nationally.

Colonial attempts to issue paper currency had long provoked British opposition, often giving rise to draconian legislation and economic regulations. The elder Adams, in order to draw upon his assets, invested in a land bank, a scheme by which paper notes were issued against his property. In 1744, the basis for his wealth vanished in an instant when, by Act of Parliament, corporations of more than six persons were outlawed. Upon graduating from Harvard, young Samuel Adams addressed a question that now held personal meaning: "Whether it be lawful to resist the supreme magistrate if the commonwealth cannot otherwise be preserved." He argued, in Latin, on behalf the right to rebel.

Opposite: A portrait of Samuel Adams, whom Thomas Jefferson called, "The helmsman of the American Revolution."

Below: Samuel Adams, like many of his fellow Founding Fathers, attended Harvard College, seen here in a Paul Revere engraving after a drawing by Joseph Chadwick.

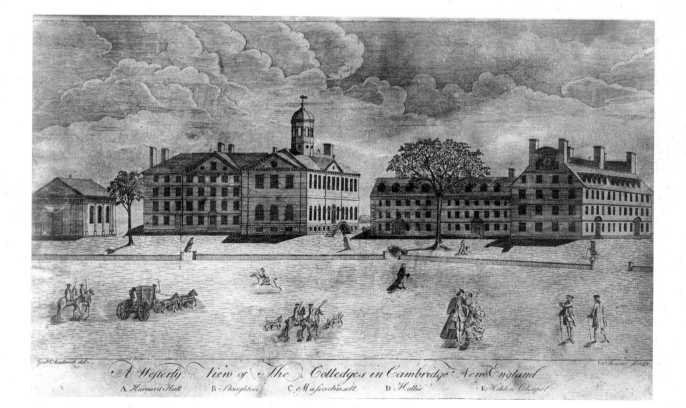

After the death of his father, Adams assumed management of the brewery. It had never been overly profitable, and Adams spent more time fending off creditors than brewing beer. During this period Adams showed a passion for political discourse, in one instance calling for the Massachusetts General Court to have the final word on colonial matters, a proposal that found few adherents. In 1756, Adams became Boston's tax collector, a post that enabled him to cultivate allies and offset the many powerful enemies he had made. In 1764, he drafted Boston's response to the Stamp Act, the first public protest in America against the right of parliament to tax the colonies. The next year, Adams was elected to the legislature and served as clerk. Thereafter, he issued petitions and letters of instruction, most notably his circular letter sent in February 1768 to the assemblies of the other colonies asking them to support Massachusetts in its resistance to paying the taxes and import duties imposed on them without representation in Parliament.

Shocked by the Boston Massacre of 1770, in which British troops fired upon a Boston crowd, killing several, many looked to Adams for a response. He chaired a citizen committee that demanded the removal of the two British regiments then stationed in Boston. Offered the removal of one regiment, Adams insisted, "Both regiments or none," a position that won wide support.

As general indignation over British rule gathered force, and with the colonial governor increasingly unresponsive, Adams proposed a new form of representation. The Committees of Correspondence would give citizens the opportunity to express discontent and seek remedy. Within

ABOVE: *The Boston Tea Party, as seen from the docks in a painting by the eighteenth century Polish–German artist Daniel Chodowiecki. Samuel Adams was said to be one of the protesters who, dressed as a Native American, boarded British ships in Boston Harbor and threw cargoes of tea overboard.*

months many Massachusetts towns had such committees; soon other colonies followed suit. Out of these inter-colonial Committees of Correspondence there emerged an apparatus for convening a Continental Congress, where the founding documents of independence and governance were to be forged.

In December 1773, Adams delivered an oration at Boston's Faneuil Hall that led to what would be known as the Boston Tea Party; some accounts place him on the ships, tossing tea into the harbor. The protest provoked the British to annul the colony's charter. Yet Adam's popularity was such that Governor Thomas Gage offered him a well-paid position in the administration. Although impoverished, Adams declined, whereupon Gage declared that he would pardon all citizens who agreed to cease their protests and accept British authority, but not Adams, whose "offenses [were] of too flagitious a nature."

The rest of the colonies, alarmed by events in Massachusetts, called for a Continental Congress to assemble in Philadelphia. Once a collection had been taken to pay for his journey, Adams attended the First Continental Congress in 1774. In Philadelphia Adams encountered resistance to his brand of Massachusetts radicalism, so he exercised restraint and practiced

BELOW: *Samuel Adams gave fiery speeches at Faneuil Hall (center, with steeple) and at Old South Meeting House in Boston where he declared, "This meeting can do nothing more to save this country." His words sparked the Boston Tea Party.*

Circular Letter from the Massachusetts House of Representatives to the Speakers of other Colonies' Legislatures
February 11, 1768

SIR,

The House of Representatives of this Province have taken into their serious consideration, the great difficulty that must accrue to themselves & their Constituents, by the operation of several acts of Parliament imposing Duties & Taxes on the American Colonys.

As it is a Subject in which every Colony is deeply interested they have no reason to doubt but your Assembly is deeply impressd with its Importance & that such constitutional measures will be come into as are proper. It seems to be necessary, that all possible Care should be taken, that the Representations of the several Assembly upon so delicate a point, should harmonize with each other: The House therefore hope that this letter will be candidly considerd in no other Light, than as expressing a Disposition freely to communicate their mind to a Sister Colony, upon a common Concern in the same manner as they would be glad to receive the Sentiments of your or any other House of Assembly on the Continent.

The House have humbly represented to the ministry, their own Sentiments that His Majestys high Court of Parliament is the supreme legislative Power over the whole Empire: That in all free States the Constitution is fixd;...That the Constitution ascertains & limits both Sovereignty & allegiance, & therefore, his Majestys American Subjects who acknowledge themselves bound by the Ties of Allegiance, have an equitable Claim to the full enjoymt of the fundamental Rules of the British Constitution....

It is moreover their humble opinion, which they express with the greatest Deferrence to the Wisdom of the Parliament that the Acts made there imposing Duties on the People of this province with the sole & express purpose of raising a Revenue, are Infringments of their natural & constitutional Rights because as they are not represented in the British Parliamt His Majestys Commons in Britain by those Acts grant their Property without their consent....

These are the Sentiments & proceedings of this House; & as they have too much reason to believe that the Enemys of the Colonys have represented them to his Majestys Ministers & the parlt as factious disloyal & having a disposition to make themselves independent of the Mother Country, they have taken occasion in the most humble terms to assure his Majesty & his ministers that with regard to the People of this province & as they doubt not of all the colonies the charge is unjust....

This House cannot conclude without expressing their firm Confidence in the King our common head & Father, that the united & dutifull Supplications of his distressd American Subjects will meet with his royal & favorable Acceptance.

---

conciliation. The following winter, the British ministry issued an order for his arrest. In April 1775, when British troops moved forth from Boston to engage the Minutemen at Concord and Lexington, Adams escaped arrest and fled to Philadelphia and the Second Continental Congress, where he helped frame the Declaration of Independence. In acknowledgment of his contributions, Thomas Jefferson called Adams "the helmsman of the American Revolution."

ABOVE: *Samuel Adams, along with Paul Revere, led the Sons of Liberty, a radical group that fought for independence through a variety of means, including violence. In a drawing by Philip Dawe, a mob forces loyalists to sign non-importation agreements at the threat of public tar and feathering.*

For the next eight years, Adams served in the Continental Congress, helping steer the new nation through the difficult years of Revolution. In time, Adams aligned with the Anti-Federalists in opposition to a strong central government. Although he recognized the imperfections of the Articles of Confederation, he argued for their amendment. However, once the new constitution was drafted in 1787, Adams campaigned for ratification, with an important condition: freedoms of speech and press and the right to bear arms must be protected. His support was critical for ratification to pass, narrowly, at the Massachusetts Convention. The freedoms he had defended during the ratification debate were formalized in the Bill of Rights in 1791.

In 1789 Adams was appointed lieutenant governor of Massachusetts and inherited the governorship in 1794. He won reelection until retirement in 1797. Although his name was put forward as a vice presidential hopeful, it was his second cousin John, a Federalist, who was selected and became the nation's second president in 1797. During his cousin's administration, Samuel Adams leaned more toward Jeffersonian republicanism. To that end, he questioned the constitutional ambiguities of the Tenth Amendment delegating all unspecified authority to the federal government. Adams remained consistent in his dedication to individual liberty, and his influence was felt throughout each stage of the nation's founding, from protest to rebellion to governance.

Patrick Henry

1736–1799

Patrick Henry, the most passionate and often-quoted orator of the Revolutionary era, was a man of many paradoxes. Widely believed to have come from humble origins, Henry was, in fact, born into the Virginia gentry. And although remembered and revered for his famous call to resistance—"I know not what course others may take, but as for me—give me liberty or give me death!"—Henry may not have actually used this wording and there is evidence that the quotation was composed and edited after the fact. And although this fiery rhetoric forever gave Patrick Henry his reputation as an uncompromising revolutionary, his personal and political careers were far less radical.

Die Americaner wiedersetzen sich der
Stempel Acte, und verbrennen das aus
England nach America gesandte Stempel-
Papier zu Boston, im August 1764.

Educated under the guidance of his Scottish-born father, who had attended King's College, University of Aberdeen (Scotland), Henry turned to the study of law after failing to succeed at a number of attempts as a shopkeeper. Self-taught and poorly prepared, he managed to gain admission to the bar and soon developed a successful law practice. In the trial that came to be known as the *Parson's Cause* (1763), Henry displayed the passion and eloquence that was to mark his career. The case revolved around a Virginia law stating that for the purposes of calculating the pay of the clergy of the established Anglican Church, tobacco would be valued at two pence per pound (and clerical salaries were fixed at a specific tobacco poundage). This rate was below the market value of tobacco, and the increasingly unpopular Virginia clergy protested to King George III, who disallowed the act. The clergy then sued for back salary. In a wide-ranging defense that invoked "certain inalienable rights" and criticized the king's intervention, Henry argued the test case against one cleric's claim so successfully that the jury limited its award to one penny.

Having established himself as a defender of the rights of Virginians against infringements by the Crown, Henry soon won election to the Virginia House of Burgesses, which passed his Stamp Act Resolves in opposition to the Stamp Act of 1765. In a near legendary account of his thundering yet elegant orations against the king, Henry is reported to have threatened: "Caesar had his Brutus; Charles the First his Cromwell, and George III....(at which point he was interrupted by cries of "Treason! Treason!"), "....may profit from their example. If *this* be treason, make the most of it."

A member of the Virginia Committee of Correspondence, which promoted cooperation between the colonies, Henry was also a delegate to the Continental Congresses of 1774 and 1775. He roused the Continental Congress of 1774 by sweeping aside colonial differences with the words: "The distinctions between Virginians, Pennsylvanians, New Yorkers, and New Englanders are no more. I am not a Virginian, but an American." On March 23, 1775, as a delegate to the second Virginia Convention, arguing for resolutions to equip the Virginia militia to fight against the British, Henry made his famous "liberty or death" declaration, which moved popular opinion throughout the colonies more strongly toward independence.

Although unsuccessful as commander of the Virginia military forces during the Revolutionary war, Henry helped draft the first constitution of Virginia and served three consecutive one-year terms (1776–79) as the state's first governor. As a leading force in Virginia politics during the years after the Revolution, Henry revealed that his earlier, apparently radical positions were actually those of a staunch defender of the rights of states and individuals. Thus, he opposed efforts to strengthen the Articles of Confederation and, despite his 1763 courtroom triumph against the Anglican clergy of Virginia, he opposed its provision for separation of church and state and favored continuation of public taxation for the support of recognized religions.

Signaling his growing opposition to those who would become the Federalists, in 1785 Henry became angry at John Jay for failing in his negotiations with Spain to get Spain to cede vital navigation rights on the southern Mississippi to American shipping. He did not attend the Constitutional Convention in 1787 and opposed adoption of the Constitution at the Virginia

BELOW: *Patrick Henry delivers a speech before the Virginia Assembly on March 23, 1775, that would become a rallying cry for the Revolution in this Currier and Ives lithograph.*

PUBLISHED BY CURRIER & IVES   Entered according to act of Congress in the year 1876 by Currier & Ives in the Office of the Librarian of Congress in Washington.   152 NASSAU ST. NEW YORK

"GIVE ME LIBERTY, OR GIVE ME DEATH!"

Address to the Richmond Assembly
March 23, 1775

No man thinks more highly than I do of the patriotism, as well as abilities, of the very worthy gentlemen who have just addressed the House. But different men often see the same subject in different lights; and, therefore, I hope it will not be thought disrespectful to those gentlemen if, entertaining as I do opinions of a character very opposite to theirs, I shall speak forth my sentiments freely and without reserve. This is no time for ceremony. The questing before the House is one of awful moment to this country. For my own part, I consider it as nothing less than a question of freedom or slavery; and in proportion to the magnitude of the subject ought to be the freedom of the debate. It is only in this way that we can hope to arrive at truth, and fulfill the great responsibility which we hold to God and our country. Should I keep back my opinions at such a time, through fear of giving offense, I should consider myself as guilty of treason towards my country, and of an act of disloyalty toward the Majesty of Heaven, which I revere above all earthly kings....

The battle, sir, is not to the strong alone; it is to the vigilant, the active, the brave. Besides, sir, we have no election. If we were base enough to desire it, it is now too late to retire from the contest. There is no retreat but in submission and slavery! Our chains are forged! Their clanking may be heard on the plains of Boston! The war is inevitable—and let it come! I repeat it, sir, let it come.

It is in vain, sir, to extenuate the matter. Gentlemen may cry, Peace, Peace—but there is no peace. The war is actually begun! The next gale that sweeps from the north will bring to our ears the clash of resounding arms! Our brethren are already in the field! Why stand we here idle? What is it that gentlemen wish? What would they have? Is life so dear, or peace so sweet, as to be purchased at the price of chains and slavery? Forbid it, Almighty God! I know not what course others may take; but as for me, give me liberty or give me death!

Convention. In a foreshadowing of later divisions between North and South, Henry warned the rights of the states were not adequately protected. Most important, Henry was unconvinced that individual rights would be properly guarded. For once, his oratory was not successful. His fellow Virginian John Marshall observed that although Henry might be the great oratorical champion in his ability to persuade, Madison was his superior in his capacity to convince. Only after the passage of the Bill of Rights did Henry become reconciled to Virginia's ratification of the Constitution. Despite his reputation as a strong advocate of states' rights, in 1799 Henry came out of political retirement to oppose the Kentucky and Virginia Resolutions, which claimed that states could determine the constitutionality of federal laws. His final speech was a passionate plea for American unity.

Although he never held high national office and his positions were inconsistent, and sometimes at odds with the prevailing majority, the passion and commitment of Patrick Henry's voice constantly fueled the Revolution and resonate among the words of the Founding Fathers.

Benjamin Franklin

1706–1790

As the most famous American both throughout the colonies, and abroad, distinguished as a printer, publisher, writer, philosopher, scientist, diplomat, and civic innovator, Benjamin Franklin was the embodiment of American enlightenment, self-reliance, and democratic genius. Although a visionary, constantly devising radical new ideas and concepts, Franklin was valued by the Founding Fathers for his prudent counsel and ability to forge sensible compromise.

The twelfth child of a Boston candle maker who came to New England to practice his Puritan faith, Franklin received little formal education and at the age of twelve, was apprenticed as an indentured laborer to an older half-brother, a printer. Secular, intellectually inquisitive, and fun-loving, Franklin taught himself the elements of literary style, and at the age of fifteen, launched his long career as a writer with a series of satirical essays he published anonymously in *The New England Courant*. In 1722, after his brother's arrest for criticizing local government officials in his newspaper, the teenage Franklin managed *The New England Courant* during his brother's imprisonment, eluded attempts at censorship, and continued to publish his increasingly popular essays. The following year, Franklin fled both puritanical Boston and his confining lot as an apprentice, and made his way to Philadelphia.

Encouraged by the more liberal atmosphere he found there, Franklin undertook a journey to England in 1724 to purchase printing equipment needed to set up his own press in Philadelphia. After a year in London, where he circulated among the city's free-thinkers and printed clandestine editions for his radical friends, Franklin returned to Philadelphia and established himself as a successful merchant and printer. His belief in a free and flourishing press as prerequisite to the development of an inventive society was rooted in these early experiences.

During the next decade, Franklin founded America's first subscription library; campaigned for the issuing of paper currency in Pennsylvania; devised a method to print bills (reproducing images of plant leaves) that would thwart counterfeiters; proposed and organized the first fire society; founded the precursor of the University of Pennsylvania; became librarian

Benjamin Franklin's Answers to Questions from the House of Commons
February 15, 1766

Q. What was the temper of America toward Great Britain before the year 1763?

A. The best in the world. They submitted willingly to the government of the Crown, and paid, in their courts, obedience to acts of Parliament. Numerous as the people are in the several old provinces they cost you nothing in forts, citadels, garrisons, or armies, to keep them in subjection. They were governed by this country at the expense only of a little pen, ink, and paper; they were led by a thread. They had not only a respect but an affection for Great Britain; for its laws, its customs, and manners, and even a fondness for its fashions, that greatly increased the commerce. Natives of Britain were always treated with particular regard; to be an Old England-man was of itself a character of some respect, and gave a kind of rank among us.

Q. And what is their temper now?

A. Oh, very much altered!

Q. Can anything less than a military force carry the Stamp Act into execution?

A. I do not see how a military force can be applied to that purpose.

Q. Why may it not?

A. Suppose a military force sent into America: they will find nobody in arms; what are they then to do? They can not force a man to take stamps who chooses to do without them. They will not find a rebellion; they may, indeed, make one.

Q. If the Stamp Act should be repealed, and the Crown should make assemblies of America to acknowledge the rights of Parliament to tax them, and would they erase their resolutions?

A. No, never!

Q. Are there no means of obliging them to erase those resolutions?

A. None that I know of; they will never do it, unless compelled by force of arms.

Q. Is there a power on earth that can force them to erase them?

A. No power, how great soever, can force men to change their opinions.

Q. What used to be the pride of the Americans?

A. To indulge in the fashions and manufactures of Great Britain.

Q. What is now their pride?

A. To wear their old clothes over again till they can make new ones.

of the archives of the Pennsylvania Assembly; and served as postmaster of Philadelphia, using his franking privileges to establish a network of correspondence that circulated printed material to academics and community leaders throughout the colonies.

Equally important, Franklin set up partnerships and subsidiary printing presses in a number of the colonies, contributing to the independence and variety of the publishing industry in America. The publication in 1732 of *Poor Richard*, the most useful, and entertaining almanac of its time, brought Franklin's lively, intelligent persona into households throughout the colonies and beyond. His wit and homespun common sense made *Poor Richard* one of the best selling publications in the English language. Franklin's preface to the 1757 edition was reprinted under the title *The Way to Wealth*, and became a classic. His autobiography followed and received wide readership.

Franklin received his greatest international acclaim and honor as a scientist and natural philosopher. He was the first to theorize that the Atlantic seaboard's "northeaster" storms were caused by tropical storms moving up the coast from the south. He analyzed the nature of waterspouts and whirlwinds, positing that they revolved around vacuums. He observed and plotted the Gulf Stream. Most important were his experiments identifying the nature and properties of electricity, including his famous experiment with lightning and the kite in 1752.

Franklin was lionized by the public as he translated the results of his observations into practical applications such as the lightning rod and the energy efficient "Franklin stove." His scientific writings were translated into French and German. He received honorary degrees from Harvard, Yale, and the College of William and Mary and was awarded the Royal Society's Copley Medal for scientific achievement, and made a member of the Royal Society. In the 1760s he was also awarded an honorary doctor of law degree from Oxford, and was honored by universities and academies throughout Europe. Immanuel Kant pronounced Benjamin Franklin "the Prometheus of modern time."

BELOW: *An illustrated version of* Poor Richard's Almanac, *commemorating Benjamin Franklin's work and his death in 1790. Franklin published his first* Almanac *in 1732.*

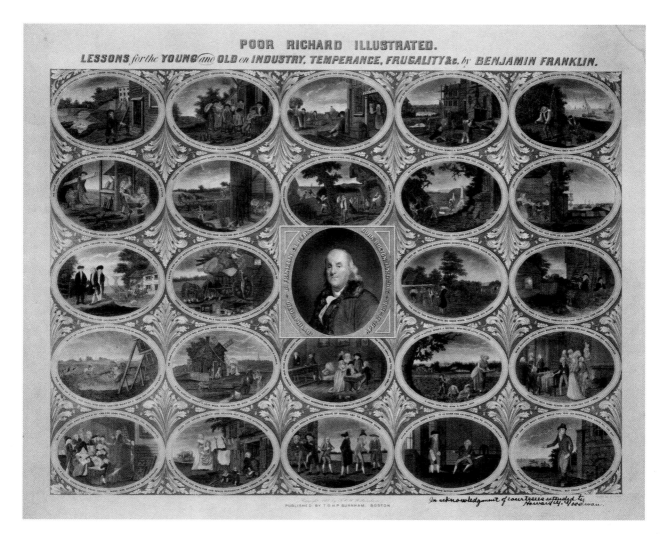

As early as the 1750s, inspired by the union of the Iroquois nations, Franklin proposed and publicized the idea of an independent union of the colonies, which he illustrated with a broadside cartoon of a snake cut into pieces, with the caption, "Join, or Die." In 1757, the Pennsylvania Assembly appointed Franklin as agent to London to represent their case for a change in the exemption of proprietary lands from general taxation. In England, Franklin led an extensive campaign to educate the British public about the economic and strategic importance of the American colonies. His *In Defense of Americans* (1759) and *The Interest of Great Britain Considered* (1760) were among his most important writings.

During his second mission as agent to London (1764–1775), the notorious Stamp Act of 1765 roused the fury of the American colonies. Torn by loyalty to England, his position as a highly honored British subject, and his long-held conviction that it was "an undoubted right of Englishmen not to be taxed but by their own Consent given thro' their Representatives," Franklin opposed the Stamp Act but counseled compliance once it was passed. Rumors that Franklin supported the Stamp Act, and that his son's appointment as governor of New Jersey had been reward for his loyalty to the Crown led to a mob attacking his house in Philadelphia. However, when word of his responses to a questioning by the British House of Commons in 1766 reached America, Franklin returned to favor.

Franklin threw himself into defense of American interests and was named agent in London for Georgia, New Jersey, and Massachusetts in addition to his position as agent for Pennsylvania. Frustrated by British refusal to consider the rights of the colonists, Franklin predicted American independence as the eventual remedy, but felt the colonies needed time to develop before attempting separation from England. After endless humiliation by British authorities, Franklin returned to America in 1775 and was appointed to the Second Continental Congress.

As leader of the most radical bloc of the Congress, in July 1775 Franklin drafted articles of confederation that outlined America's sovereignty and proposed a central government invested with greater power than that provided by the Constitution in 1787. Congress was not yet ready to adopt such measures, but Franklin continued to be involved in many of the Revolution's boldest endeavors.

LEFT: Benjamin Franklin's famous "Join, or Die" cartoon from the Pennsylvania Gazette, May 9, 1754, was based on the superstition that a snake cut in two would rejoin if the pieces were left next to each other. It is considered to be the first American political cartoon.

BELOW: A cartoon by Philip Dawe shows a patriotic barber throwing a British soldier out of his shop. The poem below reads in part, "Forbid the Captains there to roam,/Half shave them first, then send 'em home,/Objects of ridicule."

In 1776, Congress sent him on a mission to convince Canada to join the Revolution. He returned from this effort in time to help edit Jefferson's draft of the Declaration of Independence, making the list of grievances more specific, and toning down an occasional fiery phrase. As Congress debated the draft of the Declaration, and struck entire clauses, Jefferson was distraught. "I have made it a rule," Franklin consoled his youngest colleague, "whenever in my power, to avoid becoming the draughtsman of papers to be reviewed by a public body."

Elected president of the Pennsylvania state convention on July 16, 1776, he guided the convention in the adoption of the most egalitarian of all state constitutions. In a rejected draft of a bill of rights for the state of Pennsylvania, Franklin claimed that the state had a right to prevent individuals from amassing large concentrations of wealth and property, as this would be a danger to the majority. During the summer of 1776, in the congressional debates on the Articles of Confederation, Franklin argued without success for proportional, rather than equal representation of the states in Congress.

In September 1776, Congress elected Franklin one of three envoys to France with the mission of enlisting French support for the American cause. The gravity of Franklin's reputation, his wit, charm, and simplicity of style made him a sensation both among the French people and at the French Court. Although criticized in America for his apparently meandering approach to his mission, Franklin achieved what no one else could possibly have accomplished. When John Adams, frustrated by Franklin's oblique style of diplomacy, approached the French foreign minister with direct demands for aid, he was told that the minister would no longer receive communications from Adams. Through patience, shrewdness, bluff, and personal charisma, Franklin managed to obtain small but meaningful French assistance during the early months of the war, when Washington's armies were in retreat. After the British surrendered at Saratoga in October 1777, Franklin was able to secure far more substantial aid from France.

LEFT: *Writing the Declaration of Independence by Jean Leon Gerome Ferris. Benjamin Franklin, John Adams, and Thomas Jefferson work on a draft of the document at Jefferson's lodgings at the corner of Seventh and High (Market) Streets in Philadelphia.*

RIGHT: *Benjamin Franklin being received by the French Court, including the seated Louis XIV and Marie Antoinette. Franklin's rapport with the French was instrumental in winning Gallic support for the American cause during the Revolution.*

BELOW: *The eighty-one-year-old Benjamin Franklin delivering a speech before the Constitutional Convention. An advocate of a strong central government, Franklin signed the Constitution as a representative of Pennsylvania.*

With John Jay and John Adams, who joined him in Paris, Franklin presided over the peace negotiations that resulted in the Treaty of Paris of 1783, which ended the war between America and England and recognized American independence. If Jay had not delayed the start of negotiations with preconditions, Franklin might have secured Canada for the Americans, but in the interim Britain's position with regard to France strengthened. Franklin was never idle. Most famous of his inventions during the months spent negotiating the Treaty of Paris was the concept of bifocal lenses.

Returning to America in 1785, Franklin was one of Pennsylvania's delegates to the Constitutional Convention. Franklin supported the Great Compromise, providing for proportional representation according to the population of each state in the House of Representatives, but equality for each state in the Senate. He also argued for extending the right to vote and hold office as widely as possible. Although Franklin did not approve of everything in the Constitution, he signed it and urged its adoption.

Now eighty-one years old, Franklin returned to his home in Philadelphia. His final effort, typically visionary in scope, was a proposal to Congress that would outlaw slave trade and slavery in the newly formed nation. By the time of his death in 1790, Washington may have emerged as the most respected American, but Benjamin Franklin remained unrivaled as the most genial, versatile, and ubiquitous of the Founding Fathers.

John Hancock

1737–1793

With his oversized signature, outsized ego, outrageous good fortune and out-and-out genius at catering to the public will, John Hancock was a larger-than-life Founding Father.

Born in Braintree (now Quincy), Massachusetts, the son of a minister, John moved to his grandfather's house at age seven after his father died, then almost immediately relocated to live with his with uncle and aunt Thomas and Lydia Hancock of Boston. A leading merchant, Thomas Hancock eyed his nephew as a possible successor for he and his wife had no children. After graduating from Boston Latin High School and Harvard College (where he was punished for drinking and missing chapel), John joined the business amid overflowing government orders during the final French and Indian War. As his uncle's health declined, Hancock took greater control over duties like acquiring and selling real estate, negotiating government contracts and exporting whale oil. While building his business,

Nº VII] *Engraved for the* MASSACHUSETTS MAGAZINE, *July 1789.* [VOL. I.

Oration in Commemoration of the Boston Massacre
March 5, 1774

But I forbear and come reluctantly to the transactions of that dismal night [of the Boston Massacre]..., when Heaven, in anger for a dreadful moment, suffered Hell to take the reins; when Satan, with his chosen band, opened the sluices of New England's blood and sacrilegiously polluted our land with the dead bodies of her guiltless sons...Let all American join in one common prayer to Heaven that the inhuman unprovoked murders of the fifth of March 1770, planned by Hillsborough and a knot of treacherous knaves in Boston and executed by the cruel hand

of Preston and his sanguinary coadjutators, may ever stand on history without a parallel!...

[B]y all that is honorable, by all that is sacred, [I ask] not only that ye pray, but that you act; that if necessary, ye fight, and even die for the prosperity of our Jerusalem.... Despise the glare of wealth! The people who pay greater respect to a wealthy villain than to an honest, upright man in poverty almost deserve to be enslave; they plainly show that wealth, however it may be acquired, is, in their esteem, to be preferred to virtue...

LEFT: *A 1777 article from Bickerstaff's Boston Almanack honoring John Hancock as a patriot and as the president of the Continental Congress.*

he gave free Bibles to poor churches and allowed poor debtors to pay with depreciated paper notes while making wealthy debtors pay him in silver.

In 1764, Thomas Hancock died and John took charge. At first, his timing looked terrible. When the French and Indian War ended, the debt-ridden British government began imposing tax after tax on the colonies. Although by nature a moderate, Hancock allied with patriots as a Boston selectman (1765–1774) and member of the General Court, or legislature (1766–1774). He had a natural constituency of employees, customers and debtors—at least, those whom he tolerated for supporting him politically.

Hancock's sloop *Liberty* was seized in 1768 for allegedly smuggling wine, and the Sons of Liberty forced customs agents to flee. To everyone in Boston Hancock was a victim and martyr. He was chosen to give the fourth annual (Boston) Massacre Day speech in March 1774, and he aroused an

Ye dark, designing knaves; ye murderers, parricides! How dare you tread upon the earth which has drank in the blood of slaughtered innocence shed by your wicked hands? How dare you breathe that air which wafted to the ear of heaven the groans of those who fell a sacrifice to your accursed ambition? But if the laboring earth dot not expand her jaws; if the air you breathes is not commissioned to be the minister of death; yet hear it and tremble! The eye of Heaven penetrates the darkest chambers of the sol.... and you...must be arraigned, must lift your hands, red with blood of those whose death you procured, at the tremendous bar of God.

But I thank God that America abounds in men who are superior to all temptation.... And sure I am I should not incur your displeasure if I paid respect so justly due to their much honored characters in this public place; but when I name an Adams [Samuel] such a numerous host of fellow patriots rush upon my mind that I fear I would take up too much of your time should I attempt to call over the illustrious roll.

BELOW: *A 1768 engraving by Paul Revere illustrating the arrival of British warships in Boston Harbor where John Hancock's sloop* Liberty *was seized by customs agents that same year for allegedly smuggling wine.*

overflow crowd at the Old South Meeting House with a stirring oration (which most scholars believe he had a great deal of help in composing). Coming just three months after the Boston Tea Party, the speech thrust him to the forefront of patriot ranks. Hancock was named president of the Provincial Congress in 1774 and a delegate to the Second Continental Congress in Philadelphia in 1775. Before heading there, he moved for safety reasons to his grandfather's old house in Lexington, where he and Samuel

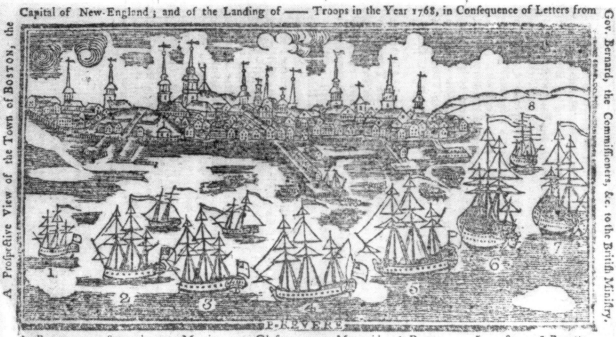

Adams heard Paul Revere's warning of approaching British troops. After the battles of Lexington and Concord, Hancock and Adams headed to Philadelphia.

The Congress convened in May, and Hancock landed as president after the first presiding officer returned home on business and his replacement resigned for health reasons. With the advantages of his progressive views, wealth and social standing, Hancock was elected unanimously. That was not enough honor for Hancock, who expected to be named commander in chief of the Continental army despite no qualifications whatsoever.

After adjournment in August 1775, Hancock returned home, then married Dorothy Quincy in Connecticut on his way back to Philadelphia a few weeks later. Though he did little more than to preside, Hancock made a splash as one of only two signers of the Declaration of Independence on July 4—the rest signed on August 2—and the one whose signature would be the largest. According to a popular but unconfirmed story, Hancock's name was written large so that the king of England could read it without his glasses. In any case, signatories are still asked to "put your John Hancock" on documents.

Below: A Currier and Ives lithograph, which helped to promulgate the story that a defiant John Hancock signed his name extra large so "John Bull" could read it without spectacles.

PUBLISHED BY CURRIER & IVES

Robt. Morris.   Saml. Adams   Benjamin Rush   Charles Carroll   Rev. John Witherspoon.   John Adams   John Hancock   Edwd. Rutledge.
Richard Henry Lee

Engraved according to act of Congress Congress in the year 1876 by Currier & Ives, in the Office of the Librarian of Congress at Washington.   152 NASSAU ST NEW YORK

JOHN HANCOCK'S DEFIANCE.

JULY 4TH 1776.

The Declaration of Independence being fully adopted, John Hancock, President of the Continental Congress took up the pen and signed his name to it in a large bold hand; then rising he said, "There! John Bull can read

Puritanical New England delegates were offended by his extravagance. Nonetheless, he was overwhelmingly elected the first governor of Massachusetts after it adopted its constitution in 1780. A natural politician, Hancock took moderate positions, supported widows, orphans, and other needy constituents and was easily re-elected. In 1785 he resigned, citing health reasons but doubtless aware that the state's economy was crumbling and returning soldiers were overburdened by property and poll taxes they couldn't pay with their worthless wartime scrip. Hancock's successor as governor, James Bowdoin, inherited the odious task of suppressing Shays's Rebellion (1786–87). In its aftermath, Hancock's health magically returned and he whipped Bowdoin to return as governor. He gave limited pardons to most of the rebels and engineered tax relief.

His greatest moment still lay ahead. When the national Constitution was sent to Massachusetts for ratification on January 2, 1788, anti-government forces outside Boston clashed with pro-government delegates from the capital region. Named president of the convention, Hancock waited until January 31, then delivered a speech given credit for winning ratification by a vote of 187-168. Motives aside, Hancock influenced a pivotal state and correctly added a coda to his speech: that a bill of rights was still needed to curb an overzealous central government.

Hancock was disappointed to be passed over as George Washington's vice president, but he remained governor of Massachusetts until his death in 1793. Whatever else could be said about Hancock, when opportunity knocked he always strode through the right door. His conciliatory instincts made him an ideal presiding officer, and his role in securing both independence and a constitutional republic was as large as his signature style.

Part Two

Fighting for Freedom

(1776—1783)

Although the Second Continental Congress that convened in May 1775 voted to raise an army under George Washington—explaining this in the declaration of July 1775—most of the colonists were far from ready to take up arms against their British "cousins." Many, in fact, would be so opposed to the actions endorsed by the Continental Congress in the months ahead that they would proclaim themselves loyalists; some would stay on during the revolutionary conflict and try to keep a low profile, but many fled to Great Britain or Canada or other British possessions. Not even all the delegates to the Congress were ready to make a complete break from Great Britain. John Dickinson, for example, even though he had for a decade or more been opposing many of the actions of the British government, came to Philadelphia advocating a peaceful settlement of their disputes.

The president of this Second Continental Congress was John Hancock, the wealthy Boston merchant who had become one of Samuel Adams's most devoted colleagues. Under Hancock, the Congress proceeded to vote for establishing a navy and a group known as the Continental Marines as well as to issue money to pay for what was now accepted as a war. They also endorsed a plan to take control of Canada—a plan that came to disaster on December 31, 1775, when American forces suffered a crushing defeat in an attempt to take Quebec City. More successful was the epic transfer of some sixty cannon and mortars from the recently captured British Fort Ticonderoga to the high ground surrounding Boston, thus placing the British troops there under siege.

PREVIOUS PAGE: A detail of The Declaration of Independence, by artist John Trumbull, depicting the signing of the great document. Trumbull took some artistic liberties, imagining a grand event with all signers in attendance.

ABOVE: John Adams addresses the Continental Congress in Philadelphia, nominating George Washington as commander in chief of the Continental army, in a painting by John Ward Dunsmore.

Richard Henry Lee
Resolution Introduced at Second Continental Congress
June 7, 1776

Resolved, That these United Colonies are, and of right ought to be, free and independent States, that they are absolved from all allegiance to the British Crown, and that all political connection between them and the State of Great Britain is, and ought to be, totally dissolved.

That it is expedient forthwith to take the most effectual measures for forming foreign Alliances.

That a plan of confederation be prepared and transmitted to the respective Colonies for their consideration and approbation.

RIGHT: *An engraving by Jean Jacques François Lebarbier depicting the funeral of Richard Montgomery, an American brigadier general who was killed in the battle for Québec City. The battle was fought as part of a plan to bring Canada under American control.*

BELOW: *An ornate copy of the Declaration of Independence made in 1819 and certified by then Secretary of State John Quincy Adams.*

The publication of recent immigrant Thomas Paine's *Common Sense* in February 1776 did much to boost the colonists' sense that they should go all the way and seek total freedom. But it was not until June 7, 1776, that Richard Henry Lee of Virginia introduced a resolution calling for Congress to declare its independence; on June 10, Congress voted to set up a committee to compose such a declaration. Named to this committee were John Adams, Benjamin Franklin, Richard Henry Lee, Robert R. Livingston, and Roger Sherman. Because Lee had to return to Virginia, Thomas Jefferson was named to replace him and the committee now invited Jefferson to draft a declaration. He did this during the ensuing two weeks, drawing on both his own extensive reading of European works and other similar American documents. When he was finished, he passed it by Adams and Franklin, who both made some revisions.

On July 2, the Congress finally voted to adopt Lee's resolution, and having done that, they then proceeded to debate Jefferson's draft. Again, several changes were made and on July 4, the Congress adopted the final version of the Declaration of Independence.

As president of the Congress, John Hancock signed it and it was immediately sent off to a printer. It was not until July 8 that it was read to a public gathering before the State House in Philadelphia. Congress then ordered that the Declaration be written in a fine script on parchment, and after this was completed, fifty-six members of the Congress signed it (most of them on August 2, 1776).

Whereas this might have once been treated as the first step toward founding a nation, it should be clear by now that it was at best a second phase. It had taken a lot of people, a lot of words, and a lot of actions, to get to this document. Yet, as significant as it was, much still remained to be done before a new nation was truly founded and secured. For the next five and a half years, the war raged, on sea as well as on land, and for much of that time the cause of the colonies was by no means guaranteed. There were many brave soldiers and sailors of all ranks who contributed to this struggle, but it is generally agreed that it was the personal authority and charisma of George Washington that held the colonial forces together and inspired them to continue the fight. The dismal winter of 1777 to 1778 at Valley Forge is only the most famous of the many "times that [tried] men's souls," as Thomas Paine wrote in his *American Crisis*.

And not all the heroes of this revolutionary war were on the battle lines. Benjamin Franklin went to Paris in 1776 and used every one of his personal and professional wiles to get the French government to support the American colonies' cause. When the French did sign treaties to do so in February 1778, George Washington himself was one of the first to recognize the importance of this development. Meanwhile, on the home front, men

BELOW: *When faced with cannons brought from Fort Ticonderoga by Colonel Henry Knox, the British beat a hasty retreat from Boston by ship on March 26, 1776.*

BEELER SC

EVACUATION OF BOSTON

The Articles of Confederation Ratified and in Force
March 1, 1781

PREAMBLE
To all to whom these Presents shall come, we the undersigned Delegates of the States affixed to our Names send greeting. Articles of Confederation and perpetual Union between the States of New Hampshire, Massachusetts bay, Rhode Island and Providence Plantations, Connecticut, New York, New Jersey, Pennsylvania, Delaware, Maryland, Virginia, North Carolina, South Carolina and Georgia.

Article I. The Stile of this Confederacy shall be "The United States of America."

Article II. Each state retains its sovereignty, freedom, and independence, and every power, jurisdiction, and right, which is not by this Confederation expressly delegated to the United States, in Congress assembled.

Article III. The said States hereby severally enter into a firm league of friendship with each other, for their common defense, the security of their liberties, and their mutual and general welfare, binding themselves to assist each other, against all force offered to, or attacks made upon them, or any of them, on account of religion, sovereignty, trade, or any other pretense whatever....

Article V. ...In determining questions in the United States in Congress assembled, each State shall have one vote....Freedom of speech and debate in Congress shall not be impeached or questioned in any court or place out of Congress, and the members of Congress shall be protected in their persons from arrests or imprisonments, during the time of their going to and from, and attendance on Congress, except for treason, felony, or breach of the peace....

Article XIII. Every State shall abide by the determination of the United States in Congress assembled, on all questions which by this confederation are submitted to them. And the Articles of this Confederation shall be inviolably observed by every State, and the Union shall be perpetual; nor shall any alteration at any time hereafter be made in any of them; unless such alteration be agreed to in a Congress of the United States, and be afterwards confirmed by the legislatures of every State....

And Whereas it hath pleased the Great Governor of the World to incline the hearts of the legislatures we respectively represent in Congress, to approve of, and to authorize us to ratify the said Articles of Confederation and perpetual Union. Know Ye that we the under-signed delegates, by virtue of the power and authority to us given for that purpose, do by these presents, in the name and in behalf of our respective constituents, fully and entirely ratify and confirm each and every of the said Articles of Confederation and perpetual Union, and all and singular the matters and things therein con-tained: And we do further solemnly plight and engage the faith of our respective constituents, that they shall abide by the determinations of the United States in Congress assembled, on all questions, which by the said Confederation are submitted to them. And that the Articles thereof shall be inviolably observed by the States we respectively represent, and that the Union shall be perpetual....

Dr. Franklin erhält, als Gesandter des
Americanischen Frey Staats, seine
erste Audienz in Frankreich, zu Versailles. am 20ten März 1778.

like Robert Livingston and Robert Morris invested their time and talents—
and in Morris's case, his private fortune—in finding ways to pay for the
costly war and to administer the logistics required to support a war.

The main hostilities ended after the British surrendered at Yorktown
on October 19, 1781, but it was September 3, 1783, before a peace treaty was
signed—a treaty negotiated largely due to the efforts of three men, John
Adams, Benjamin Franklin, and John Jay. By that time, the Continental
Congress had adopted the Articles of Confederation, effectively a constitution
for the union of the new states. As early as June 1776, the Congress had
begun considering some such arrangement, and John Dickinson quickly
drafted a document, but with the distractions of the ongoing war and the
disagreements among the delegates over the roles of their states, it was
November 15, 1777, before twelve of the thirteen states agreed to the revised
version. The one holdout was Maryland, which objected to the claims of
several of the states to the land extending far to the west. When these states
finally agreed to give up their claims, Maryland signed on March 1, 1781, at
which point the thirteen states now appeared to be a union, a nation-state.

ABOVE: *Benjamin Franklin worked
to persuade the French government to
support the cause of the American
colonies. The engraving, by Daniel
Chodowiecki, reads, "Dr. Franklin
receives, as envoy of the American free
states, his first audience with France,
at Versailles, on March 20, 1778."*

ABOVE: *Lord Charles Cornwallis surrenders at Yorktown on October 19, 1781, in a painting by John Trumbull. The surrender marked the end of the main hostilities of the Revolution.*

It remained to be seen whether the Articles of Confederation could serve as the foundation for an enduring nation-state. And once again, the individuals who had taken the lead in bringing the colonies to this stage were by no means always united in their own political thinking and goals. But it was precisely because of the give-and-take of their disagreements and debates that a strong foundation would develop.

RIGHT: *A British cartoon by James Gillray depicting the "American Rattle Snake" encircling the British troops of generals John Burgoyne and Charles Cornwallis surrendering at Saratoga and Yorktown, respectively. The snake was used as an emblem on the American flag before the stars and stripes design was implemented.*

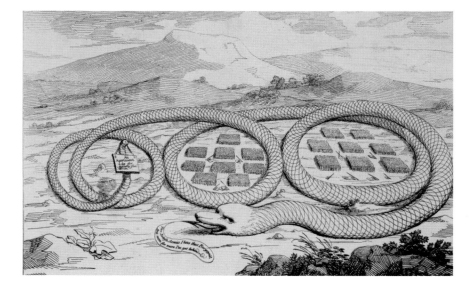

John Dickinson

1732–1808

Born in Maryland, raised in Delaware, John Dickinson provided an intellectual counterweight to New England radicalism and Hamiltonian nationalism. As his political fortunes rose and fell, he held to his principles—before the Revolution, reconciliation with Britain; after, states rights—yet also compromised, making key contributions to the nation's governing institutions. Descended from a family of tobacco farmers, Dickinson studied law at the Temple in London. He was admitted to the bar in Philadelphia where he enjoyed success. He took part in the Stamp Act Congress of 1765 and drafted resolutions and pamphlets that advanced the colonial cause. He came to hold property in both Delaware and Pennsylvania, and eventually was appointed or elected to the highest office in each state.

In 1768, his *Letters from a Farmer in Pennsylvania* made an impact on both sides of the Atlantic. The letters criticized Britain's colonial policies, yet stopped short of calling for separation. Instead, using the expertise he developed during his legal studies in London, Dickinson argued that Britain was obliged to respect the principles articulated in her own constitution, for it could not be denied that her colonies consisted of British citizens who were entitled to the rights of native-born Englishmen.

Dickinson's adherence to principle, so instrumental to his rise, would bring about his fall on the eve of the Revolution. In 1774, he joined the Continental Congress as a member from Pennsylvania. His reputation as a man of letters earned him the opportunity to draft key documents. For example, he joined Thomas Jefferson in drafting the "Declaration of Causes for Taking Up Arms," but Dickinson did not second the call for insurrection; he sought instead to moderate the document's language and arguments.

In the debates that led to the Declaration of Independence, Dickinson counseled caution. He cited the lack of a standing army, the absence of a governing structure, and the need for military support from a major power, such as France—but the revolutionary spirit carried the day. When it came for the Declaration to be signed, Dickinson declined, for to do so would be inconsistent with the position he had held. For this act of integrity, he was turned out of his seat in Congress from Pennsylvania. Delaware, however, promptly elected Dickinson to be its representative, though he did not serve until 1779.

Dickinson was not so cautious, nor so conservative, as to shirk his duty once the Revolution was underway. In 1776, he organized a battalion of militia in Philadelphia called the Associators, with whom he went to New Jersey to

Letters from a Farmer in Pennsylvania to the Inhabitants of the British Colonies

1767

My dear Countrymen,

...Let these truths be indelibly impressed on our minds—that we cannot be HAPPY, without being FREE—that we cannot be free, without being secure in our property—that we cannot be secure in our property, if, without our consent, others may, as by right, take it away—that taxes imposed on us by parliament, do thus take it away—that duties laid for the sole purpose of raising money, are taxes—that attempts to lay such duties should be instantly and firmly opposed—that this opposition can never be effectual, unless it is the united effort of these provinces—that therefore BENEVOLENCE of temper towards each other, and UNANIMITY of counsels, are essential to the welfare of the whole—and lastly, that for this reason, every man among us, who in any manner would encourage either dissension, dissidence, or indifference, between these colonies, is an enemy to himself, and to his country....

What have these colonies to ask, while they continue free? Or what have they to dread, but insidious attempts to subvert their freedom? Their prosperity does not depend on ministerial favors doled out to particular provinces. They form one political body, of which each colony is a member. Their happiness is founded on their constitution; and is to be promoted, by preserving that constitution in unabated vigor, throughout every part. A spot, a speck of decay, however small the limb on which it appears, and however remote it may seem from the vitals, should be alarming. We have all the rights requisite for our prosperity. The legal authority of Great Britain may indeed lay hard restrictions upon us; but, like the spear of Telephus, it will cure as well as wound. Her unkindness will instruct and compel us, after some time, to discover, in our industry and frugality, surprising remedies—if our rights continue unviolated: For as long as the products of our labor, and the rewards of our care, can properly be called our own, so long it will be worth our while to be industrious and frugal. But if when we plow—sow—reap—gather—and thresh—we find, that we plow—sow—reap—gather—and thresh for others, whose PLEASURE is to be the SOLE LIMITATION how much they shall take, and how much they shall leave, WHY should we repeat the unprofitable toil? Horses and oxen are content with that portion of the fruits of their work, which their owners assign them, in order to keep them strong enough to raise successive crops; but even these beasts will not submit to draw for their masters, until they are subdued by whips and goads. Let us take care of our rights, and we therein take care of our prosperity. "SLAVERY IS EVER PRECEDED BY SLEEP." Individuals may be dependent on ministers, if they please. STATES SHOULD SCORN IT—and if you are not wanting to yourselves, you will have a proper regard paid you by those, to whom if you are not respectable, you will be contemptible...

I shall be extremely sorry, if any man mistakes my meaning in any thing I have said. Officers employed by the crown, are, while according to the laws they conduct themselves, entitled to legal obedience, and sincere respect. These it is a duty to render them; and these no good or prudent person will withhold. But when these officers, through rashness or design, desire to enlarge their authority beyond its due limits, and expect improper concessions to be made to them, from regard for the employments they bear, their attempts should be considered as equal injuries to the crown and people, and should be courageously and constantly opposed. To suffer our ideas to be confounded by names on such occasions, would certainly be an inexcusable weakness, and probably an irremediable error....

A Farmer

Der Congreß erblärt die 13 vereinigten Staaten von Nord_America für in= dependent. am 4ten July 1776.

ABOVE: *An etching of the Continental Congress by Daniel Chodowiecki. The caption reads, "Congress declares the 13 United States of North America independent on July 4, 1776."*

guard against any incursion by the British army. Upon losing his seat in Congress, Dickinson resigned from the Associators and went to Delaware. In 1777 he enlisted as a private in the Delaware volunteers and was promoted to brigadier general before the year was out. Having redeemed himself, he resigned his commission and rejoined Congress to continue his political work.

Dickinson's next great project was to promote the Articles of Confederation, which he had framed in 1777, and which, after protracted and contentious debate, were ratified in 1781—with a weaker central government than he had envisioned. During the 1780s Dickinson became "president," or governor, of Delaware (1781) and Pennsylvania (1782–1785). The Confederation proved to be a flawed system of governance, so Dickinson led the Delaware delegation to the Philadelphia Convention in 1787 to frame the Constitution.

When he was well enough to be present, Dickinson's defense of state sovereignty effectively blocked James Madison and others from imposing a strong central government. He wielded considerable influence in the eventual passage of the Connecticut Compromise, later called the Great Compromise. Roger Sherman of Connecticut took the lead in promoting the compromise between the Virginia and New Jersey Plans to satisfy a majority of states, large and small. Sherman put forth the plan in July. Yet in June, a month prior to Sherman's proposal, Dickinson had offered the same plan, only to see it defeated. Once Sherman reintroduced the plan, Dickinson lent his reputation to the cause, and Sherman carried the debate. The Great Compromise affected Congress as we know it today. To protect the interests of smaller states, such as Delaware, the compromise proposed that two members from each state be appointed to the Senate; to give larger states, such as Pennsylvania their due, the compromise allowed that the House was to be proportionally representative.

Too ill to attend the signing, Dickinson's name was written on the Constitution on his behalf. Already known as the "Penman of the Revolution," Dickinson issued open letters under the name "Fabius," urging ratification. Delaware became the first state to ratify the Constitution in December 1787. Of the three founding documents, only the Articles of the Confederation bear John Dickinson's signature in his own hand, but his influence in the framing of each was profound.

Thomas Paine

1737–1809

Many would be surprised to learn that Thomas Paine, the great political pamphleteer and firebrand essayist of the American Revolution, had only lived in America for a few months before the start of the Revolution in 1775 and had actually spent his entire life very quietly in England, with little apparent interest in politics, prior to that time. Born in Thetford, England, the son of a Quaker father and an Anglican mother, Paine attended the Thetford Grammar School for seven years, and was then apprenticed to his father, who was a corset maker. Running away from his apprenticeship, he served on a privateer for several months, and lived in London during the winter of 1757 to 1758, where he attended lectures in the natural sciences, and moved in circles where logic, reason, and freedom of inquiry were prized. Over the next years, he lived in a number of small towns, working as an excise tax collector, journeyman corset maker, and assistant schoolteacher. His first wife died in childbirth; a second marriage ended in separation. In 1774, Paine was introduced to Benjamin Franklin, who was an agent representing the American colonies in London. Armed with a letter of recommendation from Franklin, Paine sailed to Philadelphia in late 1774.

LEFT: *An engraving of Thomas Paine by William Sharp. Paine posed with some of his writings, including* Rights of Man, *which he dedicated to George Washington: "I present you a small Treatise in defense of those Principles of Freedom which your exemplary Virtue hath so eminently contributed to establish."*

ABOVE: *Thomas Paine's often radical writings earned him many enemies, as illustrated by this British cartoon by James Gillray, in which a sleeping Paine is visited by three otherworldly judges. The banner above their heads reads, "The scourge inexorable, and the tort'ring hour awaits thee."*

In America, Paine was introduced to advocates of American independence, including Benjamin Rush, John Adams, and David Rittenhouse. Rush suggested Paine write a persuasive pamphlet supporting the cause, but advised against using the actual word "independence," to avoid frightening conservative elements of the population.

In January 1776, *Common Sense* appeared; its anonymous author identified only as "an Englishman." In forceful, practical style that matched its democratic political message, Paine argued, "Of more worth is one honest man to society, and in the sight of God than all the crowned ruffians that ever lived," and that "a government of our own is our natural right." The pamphlet's most quoted passages claimed, "There is something absurd in supposing a continent to be perpetually governed by an island," and that as part of the British Empire, America's future was limited; independent, its "material eminence" and greatness were certain. Paine closed with an extraordinary vision of America's potential: "We have it in our power to begin the world over again," In a world "overrun by oppression," America could become the home of freedom, "an asylum for mankind."

Common Sense soon became one of the most successful examples of political writing in history, selling over 150,000 copies. Its impact was far-reaching. Although John Adams pronounced it merely "a tolerable summary of arguments," Benjamin Franklin noted that *Common Sense* produced a "great impression" among the delegates to the Continental Congress and that it tilted the balance toward independence.

After the Declaration of Independence, Paine joined a Philadelphia militia company defending Perth Amboy, New Jersey, and, in an effort to maintain American morale during the years of war, published a series of thirteen essays on *The American Crisis*. The first *Crisis* essay, published while the forces of George Washington were in retreat across New Jersey, began with the famous words, "These are the times that try men's souls…"

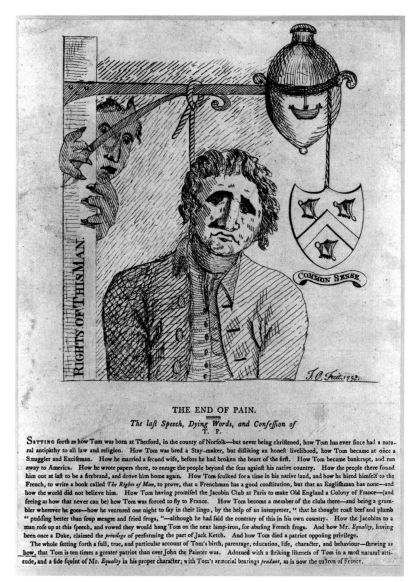

ABOVE: *A British cartoon depicting an imagined hanging of Thomas Paine. The text below the cartoon is a list of grievances with what was seen as Paine's siding with France over his native England in his book,* Rights of Man.

Throughout the years of the Revolution, Paine published essays that advocated an expanded egalitarian society in which all men could vote, a position considered radical for its time. He was involved in drafting a new constitution for Pennsylvania that allowed all men who paid taxes to vote; eliminated the office of governor; abolished imprisonment for debt; and provided for the establishment of public schools with low fees. Paine published a series of essays on economics in which he argued that unfettered commerce would produce prosperity in which all classes would share; and that a central, federal government and a central financial institution were necessary for promoting American economic development. After the war, the New York legislature awarded Paine the confiscated estate of a loyalist in New Rochelle, New York.

In 1787, Paine returned to Europe for several years, spending time in France and in England, where he was made an honorary member of the

Common Sense
February 14, 1776

INTRODUCTION

Perhaps the sentiments contained in the following pages, are not yet sufficiently fashionable to procure them general favor; a long habit of not thinking a thing wrong, gives it a superficial appearance of being right, and raises at first a formidable outcry in defence of custom. But tumult soon subsides. Time makes more converts than reason....

The cause of America is, in a great measure, the cause of all mankind. Many circumstances have, and will arise, which are not local, but universal, and through which the principles of all lovers of mankind are affected, and in the event of which, their affections are interested. The laying a country desolate with fire and sword, declaring war against the natural rights of all mankind, and extirpating the defenders thereof from the face of the earth, is the concern of every man to whom nature hath given the power of feeling; of which class, regardless of party censure, is The Author....

In the following pages I offer nothing more than simple facts, plain arguments, and common sense; and have no other preliminaries to settle with the reader, than that he will divest himself of prejudice and prepossession, and suffer his reason and his feelings to determine for themselves; that he will put on, or rather that he will not put off the true character of a man, and generously enlarge his views beyond the present day....

Volumes have been written on the subject of the struggle between England and America. Men of all ranks have embarked in the controversy, from different motives, and with various designs; but all have been ineffectual, and the period of debate is closed. Arms, as the last resource, decide the contest; the appeal was the choice of the king, and the continent hath accepted the challenge....

Society for Constitutional Information, a group that advocated parliamentary reform. Responding to Edmund Burke's *Reflections on the Revolution in France*, between 1791 and 1792 Paine published his famous two-part work, *Rights of Man*, in which he defended the progress of events in France; elaborated on the principles of republican government; and demanded political reform linked to social programs that would eliminate the plight of the poor. This work sold over 200,000 copies and became a classic text of the British radical tradition.

While in revolutionary France in 1792, Paine was convicted *in absentia* in England for publishing seditious libel. Falling victim to factions of the French Revolution, Paine was imprisoned in Paris, where he wrote *The Age of Reason*, an attack on organized Christianity that made his name anathema to religious Christians on both sides of the Atlantic.

Paine lived out his last years in poverty in America where many resented the nature of his later writings. Benjamin Franklin once remarked to Paine, "Where liberty is, there is my country," to which Paine replied, "Where liberty is not, there is my country." Paine's unending fight for social justice and his impact on political thought during four tumultuous decades of the late eighteenth century were acknowledged by friends and opponents alike.

George Mason

1725–1792

Son of a prosperous Fairfax County, Virginia, planter, George Mason played an active, if often oppositional, role in formation of the nation's earliest political policies. A private man who liked to research issues thoroughly before taking a stand, Mason did not seek the limelight as a Founding Father, but his drafts of Virginia's constitution and declaration of rights provided a foundation for the nation's Declaration of Independence and Bill of Rights.

Mason was educated privately in Virginia, with access to the library of his uncle and guardian, the Virginia legal scholar John Mercer. Mason married Anne Eilbeck of Maryland and near the Potomac River built Gunston Hall, an exceptional example of eighteenth-century American architecture, where he lived the rest of his life and became one of the richest planters in Virginia. His first wife died in 1773 and he waited until 1780 to marry Sarah Brent. In the years before the Revolution, Mason served in the Virginia House of Burgesses (1759–1761), showing particular expertise in western territory affairs, law, and commercial matters. As treasurer of the Ohio Company from 1752 to 1792, he taught himself about colonial charters and laws, producing the influential *Extracts from the Virginia Charters, with Some Remarks Upon Them.*

In response to the colonists' furor over the British Stamp Act, in 1765 he authored as a "Virginia Planter" a letter to London's merchants demanding equal treatment for the colonies and warning that "such another experiment as the Stamp-Act wou'd produce a general Revolt in America." After British imposition of the Townshend Acts, in 1769 Mason drafted Virginia's non-importation, or boycott, resolution, which was adopted to pressure British merchants into supporting repeal of these new taxes. He also wrote the Fairfax County Resolves in 1774, which attacked the Intolerable Acts and laid out the colonies' perspective.

After replacing George Washington in several Virginia Conventions (1775–1776), Mason was also asked to succeed him at the Continental Congress. He turned down the opportunity, but was still elected to the eleven-member Virginia Committee of Safety, formed to act as the executive head of the colony after the flight of the British governor, John Murray, Earl of Dunmore. At the time Mason wrote, "We came equals into this world and equals shall we go out of it."

In the spring of 1776, Mason immersed himself in a study of governments, corresponding with Richard Henry Lee and pursuing discussions with George Wythe and John Adams. Because of illness he did not appear at

Virginia Declaration of Rights
June 12, 1776

I That all men are by nature equally free and independent, and have certain inherent rights, of which, when they enter into a state of society, they cannot, by any compact, deprive or divest their posterity; namely, the enjoyment of life and liberty, with the means of acquiring and possessing property, and pursuing and obtaining happiness and safety.

II That all power is vested in, and consequently derived from, the people; that magistrates are their trustees and servants, and at all times amenable to them.

III That government is, or ought to be, instituted for the common benefit, protection, and security of the people, nation or community; of all the various modes and forms of government that is best, which is capable of producing the greatest degree of happiness and safety and is most effectually secured against the danger of maladministration; and that, whenever any government shall be found inadequate or contrary to these purposes, a majority of the community hath an indubitable, unalienable, and indefeasible right to reform, alter or abolish it, in such manner as shall be judged most conducive to the public weal....

V That the legislative and executive powers of the state should be separate and distinct from the judicative; and, that the members of the two first may be restrained from oppression by feeling and participating the burthens of the people, they should, at fixed periods, be reduced to a private station, return into that body from which they were originally taken, and the vacancies be supplied by frequent, certain, and regular elections in which all, or any part of the former members, to be again eligible, or ineligible, as the laws shall direct....

VIII That in all capital or criminal prosecutions a man hath a right to demand the cause and nature of his accusation to be confronted with the accusers and witnesses, to call for evidence in his favor, and to a speedy trial by an impartial jury of his vicinage, without whose unanimous consent he cannot be found guilty, nor can he be compelled to give evidence against himself; that no man be deprived of his liberty except by the law of the land or the judgement of his peers....

XI That in controversies respecting property and in suits between man and man, the ancient trial by jury is preferable to any other and ought to be held sacred.

XII That the freedom of the press is one of the greatest bulwarks of liberty and can never be restrained but by despotic governments.

XIII That a well regulated militia, composed of the body of the people, trained to arms, is the proper, natural, and safe defense of a free state; that standing armies, in time of peace, should be avoided as dangerous to liberty; and that, in all cases, the military should be under strict subordination to, and be governed by, the civil power.

XIV That the people have a right to uniform government; and therefore, that no government separate from, or independent of, the government of Virginia, ought to be erected or established within the limits thereof.

XV That no free government, or the blessings of liberty, can be preserved to any people but by a firm adherence to justice, moderation, temperance, frugality, and virtue and by frequent recurrence to fundamental principles.

XVI That religion, or the duty which we owe to our Creator and the manner of discharging it, can be directed by reason and conviction, not by force or violence; and therefore, all men are equally entitled to the free exercise of religion, according to the dictates of conscience; and that it is the mutual duty of all to practice Christian forbearance, love, and charity towards each other....

ABOVE: *Gunston Hall in Fairfax County, Virginia. George Mason built the home along the Potomac River in 1758 where it still stands today, a prime example of eighteenth-century architecture.*

the Virginia Convention until after the delegates had voted for independence. Nevertheless, he served on the organizing committee to formulate a state declaration of rights and plan of government, drafting the Declaration of Rights and the Commonwealth of Virginia's first constitution in 1776. Viewing the executive branch as the greatest threat to liberty, Mason created a state constitution that called for legislative, judicial, and executive branches and gave the lower legislative house the greatest power.

After serving in the General Assembly during the Revolution, he retired when it ended but became a Virginia delegate to the Constitutional Convention in Philadelphia in 1787. In 137 speeches there, he particularly opposed the vote to keep the executive and judiciary branches independent and to tip the balance towards a strong central government rather than states' rights. Unhappy that it did not contain a bill of rights, he refused to sign the Constitution. So opposed was he that he wrote and distributed *Objections to this Constitution of Government*. In it, he predicted, "This government will...produce a monarchy, or a corrupt, tyrannical aristocracy."

Returning to Virginia, Mason lobbied for a new federal convention to revise the Constitution. When that effort failed, he joined Patrick Henry and William Grayson in the opposition at Virginia's ratification convention in 1788. Having alienated Washington and Madison as well as many other Virginians in his home county, he won his delegate's seat in neighboring Stafford County. Although the Constitution was ratified without his vote, Mason helped author a document calling for modifications and in particular adding protections for individual rights. Not even passage of the Bill Rights and the Eleventh Amendment appeased him, and he refused to run for the Senate because of ill health. His last will and testament reflect his reluctant attitude toward public service: "I recommend it to my sons, from my own Experience in Life, to prefer the happiness of independence & a private Station to the troubles and Vexations of Public Business." Nevertheless, Mason enjoyed a reputation as the quintessential American of the Enlightenment.

Thomas Jefferson

1743—1826

No one more than Thomas Jefferson exemplifies the contradictions of belief inherent in those shaping a new nation. Most notorious of his contradictions is that Jefferson—the slaveholder many believe to have fathered children with an African-American slave Sally Hemings—also opposed slavery. This agrarian democrat, an educated and worldly man with a broad range of interests, penned the Declaration of Independence, fought for the Bill of Rights, and wrote many other works that underlie the foundation of the United States.

Born in Albemarle County, Virginia, of pioneer stock, he inherited 5,000 acres of farmland from his surveyor father at age fourteen, then attended the College of William and Mary (1760–1762). After studying law with George Wythe, Jefferson began to practice law in 1767, but turned to politics after two years. Once he was elected to Virginia's House of Burgesses (1769–1775), he never practiced law again. He quickly emerged as a leader of colonists in favor of independence, authoring resolutions that rejected England's right to tax or legislate over the colonies on the grounds of natural rights rather than the traditional legal or constitutional ones. These resolutions, with their important articulation of natural rights, became Jefferson's first published work, *A Summary View of the Rights of British America* (1774).

A renaissance man, he became an architect after educating himself in the work of Roman neoclassicist Andrea Palladio. Jefferson started in 1770 by constructing Monticello, which became the home for his wife Martha Wayles Skelton and their six children. Now in the registry of National Historic Landmarks, Monticello took forty years to complete it. Jefferson also designed the Virginia Capitol and the University of Virginia.

LEFT: *A presidential portrait of Thomas Jefferson by artist Rembrandt Peale. Jefferson holds a copy of the Declaration of Independence.*

BELOW: *A panoramic view of the University of Virginia campus. In addition to founding the institution, Thomas Jefferson also designed its original buildings, supervised construction, planned the curriculum, directed faculty recruitment, and served as its first rector.*

The Declaration of Independence
In Congress, July 4, 1776

The unanimous Declaration of the thirteen united States of America

When in the Course of human events, it becomes necessary for one people to dissolve the political bands which have connected them with another, and to assume among the powers of the earth, the separate and equal station to which the Laws of Nature and of Nature's God entitle them, a decent respect to the opinions of mankind requires that they should declare the causes which impel them to the separation.

We hold these truths to be self-evident, that all men are created equal, that they are endowed by their Creator with certain unalienable Rights, that among these are Life, Liberty and the pursuit of Happiness. That to secure these rights, Governments are instituted among Men, deriving their just powers from the consent of the governed. That whenever any Form of Government becomes destructive of these ends, it is the Right of the People to alter or to abolish it, and to institute new Government, laying its foundation on such principles and organizing its powers in such form, as to them shall seem most likely to effect their Safety and Happiness. Prudence, indeed, will dictate that Governments long established should not be changed for light and transient causes; and accordingly all experience hath shewn, that mankind are more disposed to suffer, while evils are sufferable, than to right

themselves by abolishing the forms to which they are accustomed. But when a long train of abuses and usurpations, pursuing invariably the same Object evinces a design to reduce them under absolute Despotism, it is their right, it is their duty, to throw off such Government, and to provide new Guards for their future security. Such has been the patient sufferance of these Colonies; and such is now the necessity which constrains them to alter their former Systems of Government. The history of the present King of Great Britain is a history of repeated injuries and usurpations, all having in direct object the establishment of an absolute Tyranny over these States. To prove this, let Facts be submitted to a candid world.

There then follows a list of some 26 grievances and charges against King George III, after which the declaration concludes:
In every stage of these Oppressions We have Petitioned for Redress in the most humble terms: Our repeated Petitions have been answered only by repeated injury. A Prince whose character is thus marked by every act which may define a Tyrant, is unfit to be the ruler of a free people. Nor have We been wanting in attentions to our Brittish brethren. We have warned them from time to time of attempts by their legislature to extend an unwarrantable jurisdiction over us. We have reminded them of the circumstances of our emigration and settlement here. We have

At the Second Continental Congress (1775–1777), Jefferson was named leader of the committee to draft the Declaration of Independence. Known for his eloquent writing, he was its primary author. Although it was edited by two other committee members, Benjamin Franklin and John Adams, and then somewhat modified by the Congress during its debate, this foundational document retained his imprimatur in such memorable phrases as "When in the course of human events..." and "We hold such truths to be self evident..."

appealed to their native justice and magnanimity, and we have conjured them by the ties of our common kindred to disavow these usurpations, which, would inevitably interrupt our connections and correspondence. They too have been deaf to the voice of justice and of consanguinity. We must, therefore, acquiesce in the necessity, which denounces our Separation, and hold them, as we hold the rest of mankind, Enemies in War, in Peace Friends.

We, therefore, the Representatives of the united States of America, in General Congress, Assembled, appealing to the Supreme Judge of the world for the rectitude of our intentions, do, in the Name, and by Authority of the good People of these Colonies, solemnly publish and declare, That these United Colonies are, and of Right ought to be Free and Independent States; that they are Absolved from all Allegiance to the British Crown, and that all political connection between them and the State of Great Britain, is and ought to be totally dissolved; and that as Free and Independent States, they have full Power to levy War, conclude Peace, contract Alliances, establish Commerce, and to do all other Acts and Things which Independent States may of right do. And for the support of this Declaration, with a firm reliance on the protection of divine Providence, we mutually pledge to each other our Lives, our Fortunes and our sacred Honor.

THE SIGNERS:

New Hampshire: *Josiah Bartlett, William Whipple, Matthew Thornton*

Massachusetts: *John Hancock, Samual Adams, John Adams, Robert Treat Paine, Elbridge Gerry*

Rhode Island: *Stephen Hopkins, William Ellery*

Connecticut: *Roger Sherman, Samuel Huntington, William Williams, Oliver Wolcott*

New York: *William Floyd, Philip Livingston, Francis Lewis, Lewis Morris*

New Jersey: *Richard Stockton, John Witherspoon, Francis Hopkinson, John Hart, Abraham Clark*

Pennsylvania: *Robert Morris, Benjamin Rush, Benjamin Franklin, John Morton, George Clymer, James Smith, George Taylor, James Wilson, George Ross*

Delaware: *Caesar Rodney, George Read, Thomas McKean*

Maryland: *Samuel Chase, William Paca, Thomas Stone, Charles Carroll of Carrollton*

Virginia: *George Wythe, Richard Henry Lee, Thomas Jefferson, Benjamin Harrison, Thomas Nelson, Jr., Francis Lightfoot Lee, Carter Braxton*

North Carolina: *William Hooper, Joseph Hewes, John Penn*

South Carolina: *Edward Rutledge, Thomas Heyward, Jr., Thomas Lynch, Jr., Arthur Middleton*

Georgia: *Button Gwinnett, Lyman Hall, George Walton*

Jefferson returned to Virginia's House of Delegates to find it had adopted a constitution without the democratic precepts he had proposed in his own version. He never succeeded in reforming that constitution, although he did manage to abolish by statute patrilineal practices, such as the requirement that an entire estate went to the eldest son. A firm believer in the privacy of religious belief, Jefferson also wrote the Statute of Religious Freedom in 1786, which laid the foundation for American

MONTICELLO, THE EAST PORTICO.

separation of church and state. His Bill for More General Diffusion of Knowledge went down to defeat in 1785, but provided an important standard for public education. He conveyed his deep commitment to public schooling when he wrote to his mentor George Wythe, "I think by far the most important bill in our whole code is that for the diffusion of knowledge among the people."

During the height of the Revolutionary War, Jefferson served as Virginia's governor (1779–1781). So many criticized his leadership during this crisis that the legislature voted for an inquiry, but ended up thanking him instead. Chastened by the experience, he returned to Monticello determined to leave public life and began *Notes on the State of Virginia*, a compendium of information, scientific in nature, about that state meant to enlighten foreigners, but it also contained a great deal of political commentary. Published in 1787 and often reprinted thereafter, it set a standard for such writings about America and refuted negative European stereotypes of the new nation.

ABOVE: *Thomas Jefferson spent forty years building his home, Monticello, near Charlottesville, Virginia. A self-taught architect, Jefferson had an affinity for neoclassical style.*

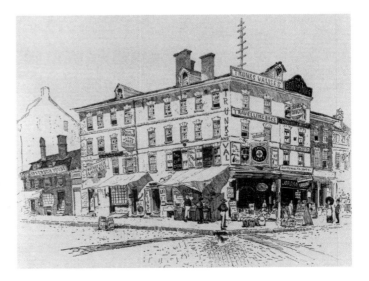

RIGHT: *A Currier and Ives lithograph modeled on the famous painting by John Trumbull, depicting Thomas Jefferson presenting the Declaration of Independence to the Continental Congress.*

The death of Jefferson's wife in 1782 brought him out of retirement, and he joined the Continental Congress in 1783. During his six-month tenure, he devised legislation for a decimal coinage system based on the dollar. His understanding, in the Ordinance of 1784, of the importance of the West, which at that time was regarded as beginning at the Appalachians, helped ensure that the western states became free, equal, and self-governing. His hopes for preventing slavery there were frustrated, though, until the 1787 Northwest Ordinance. Another contribution, the Land Ordinance of 1785, relied on Jefferson's rectilinear survey method for dividing up the western lands.

In May 1784, Jefferson left Congress for Paris to join Adams and Franklin as U.S. commissioners in European commercial treaty negotiations and then succeeded Franklin as minister to France (1785–1789). Committed to U.S. economic expansion as a counter to British trade domination, the gentleman farmer from Virginia wooed French commercial interests with help from the Marquis de Lafayette and traveled in France, England, Italy, the Netherlands, and Germany.

When Jefferson returned to the United States in 1789, he fully expected to go back to France, continuing his support for the French Revolution. Instead, newly elected President George Washington asked him to serve as secretary of state. But even before he arrived home, he had been urging that Congress add a bill of rights to the Constitution: "A bill of rights is what the people are entitled to against every government of earth, general or particular; and what no just government should refuse or rest on inferences," he wrote in 1787 to James Madison, who had sent Jefferson a copy of the new Constitution. In part due to his influence, the United States would adopt the Bill of Rights in 1791.

LEFT: *The house at Seventh and Market Streets in Philadelphia where Thomas Jefferson took two rooms, a bedroom and parlor, during the Continental Congress. In his humble parlor, Jefferson penned the Declaration of Independence.*

Jefferson also initiated negotiations with the British over the continued presence of their troops south of the Great Lakes. Convinced that economic independence from Britain played as important a role in the nation's progress as political independence, Jefferson alienated Alexander Hamilton, who as treasury secretary promoted continued economic dependence on Britain. Their deep personal antagonism reflects one of the nation's earliest schisms—between the democratic egalitarianism of Jefferson's Republican (today's Democrats) beliefs and Hamilton's aristocratically oriented Federalism. Diplomacy, rather than the threat of war, represented the keystone of Jefferson's foreign policy, and he sided with James Madison as part of the Republicans' increasingly more outspoken opposition to the governing Federalists.

A brief respite at Monticello ended when in 1796 he was drafted as the Republican presidential candidate against John Adams. He lost but became vice president, as was the policy then. Appalled by the Federalists' Alien and Sedition Acts, which he believed unconstitutional, Jefferson supported states' rights in the Kentucky Resolutions (1798) (that he authored *sub rosa*), proposing nullification, which allowed states to block enforcement of a federal law. When the 1800 presidential election deadlocked, Jefferson achieved the presidency by vote of the House of Representatives, defeating his rival Adams as well as running mate Aaron Burr.

His eloquent inaugural speech called for harmony after a bitterly contentious election campaign, and he remained a firm supporter of freedom of the press despite public attacks. Jefferson's reforms, achieved through

ABOVE: The Plundering of the King's Cellar, *an anti-French painting by Johann Zoffany depicting the 1792 storming of the Tuileries Palace in Paris. Artful propaganda like this helped to turn many Americans against the French Revolution, although Thomas Jefferson remained an avid supporter.*

ABOVE: *The committee charged with drafting the Declaration of Independence. From left to right: Thomas Jefferson, John Adams, Benjamin Franklin, Robert Livingston, and Roger Sherman.*

RIGHT: *A somewhat bizarre anti-Jefferson political cartoon by James Akin, specifically critical of the Louisiana Purchase. Jefferson is depicted as a skinny dog being stung by a Napoleon-headed hornet and coughing up two million gold dollars before a dancing Frenchman.*

nonpartisanship and negotiation rather than confrontation, led his election to be called "the revolution of 1800." He reduced the army and navy and worked to pay off the national debt, but his biggest fights came with the judicial branch, which the Federalists had tried to pack with new positions. Although he was a strict constructionist and doubted its constitutionality, Jefferson approved of the Louisiana Purchase and personally initiated the Lewis and Clark expedition.

Jefferson faced new challenges during his second term. Britain's belligerent impressment of American sailors and attack on U.S. ships edged the nation perilously close to war. Jefferson pushed instead for passage of the highly unpopular Embargo Act in 1807. The great idealist retired to Monticello for good in 1809, serving as president of the American Philosophical Society until 1815. That same year he sold his 6,000-volume library to reconstitute the Library of Congress, which had been largely destroyed when the British burned Washington in the War of 1812.

His last years saw him complete *The Life and Morals of Jesus of Nazareth*, a New Testament analysis, and lobby for a public education system in Virginia. He was only partially successful in that, but his efforts resulted in the formation of the University of Virginia. Like John Adams, with whom he had resumed his friendship and established a memorable correspondence, he died on July 4, 1826, fifty years after the adoption of the Declaration of Independence. Both a scientist and a man of the arts, Jefferson's multifaceted brilliance as a political thinker, his eloquence as a writer, his support of public education and commitment to diplomacy over war, make him one of the most humane of the Founding Fathers.

The PRAIRIE DOG sickened at the sting of the HORNET — or a Diplomatic Puppet exhibiting his Deceptions!

Caesar Rodney

1728—1784

On July 4, 1776, a vote was taken that approved "the unanimous declaration of the thirteen united states of America." But if not for a dramatic midnight ride of Caesar Rodney, that Declaration of Independence might not have been unanimous.

Rodney was born near Dover in the Delaware colony in 1728. The son of a planter, Rodney entered public life as sheriff of Kent County when he was twenty-eight years old. He served in various public roles, including justice of the peace and clerk of the orphan's court, before becoming a member of the Delaware House of Assembly. In his official capacity as a representative of Delaware, Rodney attended the Stamp Act Congress in

New York in 1765. The culmination of the colonial opposition to the Stamp Act, this congress of representatives from nine colonies produced a declaration of rights, petitioning King George III and the British Parliament to repeal all taxes levied without due representation.

In 1769, Rodney was elected speaker of the Delaware House of Assembly. He also served as a brigadier general in charge of the Delaware militia. Rodney's distinguished service in both of these posts, along with his adamant support for independence, made him a natural representative of Delaware in the Second Continental Congress, alongside Thomas McKean and George Read. As the Congress discussed whether to break away from Britain, Rodney, in his capacity as a militia leader, was called away to investigate potential riots by loyalists. Rodney was still away from Philadelphia as the vote for independence neared. It was clear that there were enough votes for independence to be declared. However, the two remaining delegates from Delaware were divided—McKean was in favor, Read was against. Without a decisive vote to tip the balance, Read and McKean would cancel one another out, leaving Delaware undecided. Without Delaware, the Declaration of

RIGHT: *The First Continental Congress meets at Carpenter's Hall in Philadelphia in September 1774 in this French engraving by François Godefroy.*

Independence would not be a unanimous one. And without unanimity among the colonies, the legitimacy of the decision could fairly be questioned. The Delaware tie had to be broken.

McKean sent urgent word by messenger to Rodney in Dover, some eighty miles away. Rodney set out for Philadelphia immediately. He rode throughout the night. In a letter dated July 4, 1776, Rodney wrote to his brother, "I arrived in Congress (tho detained by thunder and rain) time enough to give my voice in the matter of Independence. It is now determined by the Thirteen United Colonies without even one dissenting Colony—We have now got through with the whole of the declaration and ordered it to be printed so that you will soon have the pleasure of seeing it."

Rodney paid for his principled action when the more conservative voters of his county refused to re-elect him that year, but after working

BELOW: *Detail of a bas relief, part of a larger statue in Wilmington, Delaware, sculpted by James Edward Kelly, honoring Caesar Rodney's ride to cast his vote for independence.*

Letter to William Killen, Chief Justice of Delaware
Trenton, January 27, 1777

...in Haslet [a mutual friend killed in battle] We know we lost a Brave, open, Honest, Sensible Man, One Who loved his Country's more than his private Interest—But While Washington Survives the great American Cause cannot Die, his Abilities Seem to be fully Equal to the public Spirit that Called him forth—History does not furnish you with a greater Piece of Generalship Than he exhibited on the day poor Haslet fell—He fought, he conquered—And if we continue to Improve the Advantages then gained, We Shall Soon put an End to the Dreadfull Controversy that Agitates and Distracts Us—And in Return have Peace, Liberty, and Safety. Heaven!

What a Glorious Figure in the Eyes of Men and Angels will the Vast America World Exhibit, in its Free Independent State. Nothing will Then be wanting but better Men and Wiser Measures to make us a happy people...

I have been perfectly well in Health Ever Since I left Home, and do Assure you that I begin to play the General most Surprisingly. I would not have you Suppose I mean the fighting General. That is a part of Duty I have not Yet been Called upon to discharge—But when called I Trust I Shall not disgrace the American cause Tis Glorious Even to Die in a Good Cause....

to raise troops for the Continental army, he was returned to the Congress in 1777 and then elected president (governor) of Delaware in 1778. His correspondence attests to his devotion to the patriots' struggle.

Although there are no known contemporary portraits of Caesar Rodney, his likeness is now familiar to many. His historic ride for independence is memorialized on the back of Delaware's state quarter as part of the U.S. Mint's program to honor the history of the fifty United States. Rodney's heroic ride for a unanimous Declaration of Independence not only solidifies his status as a Founding Father but, gives poignant meaning to the words that appear below Rodney on the quarter—*E Pluribus Unum*, "Out of Many, One."

RIGHT: *Caesar Rodney's famous ride for independence is commemorated on the back of the Delaware quarter in the U.S. Mint's series honoring the fifty states.*

Robert Morris

1734–1806

From financier, to signer, to senator, Robert Morris played an integral role in founding the United States and establishing the national treasury. It is no small irony then that the man known as the "Financier of the Revolution" spent some of his last years in debtors' prison.

Morris was born in England, the son of a tobacco merchant. He emigrated to America at the age of thirteen, only to be orphaned two years later in another tragic irony—Morris's father was killed by a wad from a cannon being fired in his honor. Morris had received some schooling in Philadelphia, but his true education began with an apprenticeship at the father and son shipping and banking firm of Charles and Thomas Willing. When Charles Willing died, Morris became a full partner in the firm at the tender age of twenty.

Morris proved to be a shrewd businessman, eventually becoming one of the most powerful and wealthy men in Philadelphia. The Stamp Act of 1765, however, directly threatened his business interests and led Morris to support the Non-Importation Resolutions, in which American merchants agreed to halt importation of British goods until Parliament repealed the taxes. But despite Morris's opposition to the Stamp Act, he did not support all-out rebellion until the Revolution began.

Morris was elected to represent Pennsylvania at the Second Continental Congress in 1775. He chose not to vote for the Declaration of Independence when it came to a vote on July 4, 1776, feeling it premature

Left: An engraving of Robert Morris by James Barton Longacre. Morris was known as the "Financier of the Revolution."

Right: A political cartoon from 1790 protests moving the capital from New York to Washington, D.C., with an interim capital in Philadelphia. A devil at the falls leading to Philadelphia beckons the ship of state, urging, "This way Bobby," referring to Morris who allegedly instigated the move.

Circular to the Governors of the States
October 19, 1781

Sir,

I am now to address you on a subject of very great Importance. I have to detail some Facts which will demand the most serious Attention from every Legislature and from every public Officer in the United States....

The various Reports which have been circulated, the Publications in several Gazettes and even Letters from some who ought to have known better, all these Things have conspired to infuse an Opinion, that every Power in Europe is favorable to us, that great Sums of Money are already advanced to us, and that still greater may be obtained. Whatever may be the Fate of my Administration, I will never be subjected to the Reproach of Falsehood or Insincerity. I therefore take the earliest Moment, in which I am permitted, to make those Communications which will give an insight into our real Situation....

I need only observe that not a Single State has acknowledged our Independence, except France...People have flattered themselves with a visionary Idea that nothing more was necessary than for Congress to send a minister abroad, and that immediately he would obtain as much money as he chose to ask for. That when he opened a Loan, hundred[s] would run to see who should have the Honor of subscribing to it, and the like. But surely a moment's Reflection should have convinced every reasonable Man, that without the clear Prospect of Repayment, People will not part with their Property....

Sir, I must speak to you most plainly. While we do nothing for ourselves, we cannot expect the Assistance of others....It is high Time to relieve ourselves from the Infamy we have already sustained, and to rescue and restore the national Credit. This can only be done by solid Revenue. Disdaining therefore those little timid Artifices, which while they postpone the Moment of Difficulty only increase the Danger and confirm the Ruin, I prefer the open Declaration to all of what is expected, and from whence it is to be drawn. To the public Creditors therefore I say, that until the States provide Revenues for liquidating the principal and interest of the public Debt, they cannot be paid; and to the States I say, that they are bound by every principle which is held sacred among men to make that Provision.

and hoping instead for a peaceful resolution with the British, but Morris revealed his inclination toward cautious pragmatism by eventually adding his signature to the document on August 2, 1776.

During the Revolutionary War, Morris was invaluable in helping to finance the Continental army. As a member of the Ways and Means Committee, he was tenacious in retaining funds from the states. With the adoption of the Articles of Confederation in 1781, Morris was appointed superintendent of finance, and immediately began to address the dire financial situation of the new government. He established the Bank of North America, the first financial institution chartered by the United States. Morris did not hesitate to send a letter to all the states' governors that spoke honestly about the debt problem and the need to impose taxes. On occasion, he also risked his own credit and personal fortune in order to continue supplying the army with arms and equipment. But Morris's work for the government was not without controversy. While serving as superintendent of finance, Morris retained his business interests and indeed secured government contracts for his own firm. Thomas Paine, among others, accused him of profiteering during the war, but a congressional committee cleared Morris and his firm of the charges.

In 1787, Morris became one of only two men to sign all three of the seminal documents that went into founding the United States: the Declaration of Independence, the Articles of Confederation, and the United States Constitution. President George Washington nominated him to be secretary of treasury, but Morris declined, leaving the position to Alexander Hamilton. Morris instead was elected to the U.S. Senate in 1789, serving until 1795, where he generally sided with the Federalists in supporting a strong central government.

After leaving the Senate, Morris began a period of ill-advised land speculation, where he risked and eventually lost his entire fortune. In 1798 Morris, a man considered to be one of the key founders of the national treasury, was arrested for debt and spent the next several years in debtors' prison in Philadelphia. His release came only after Congress passed bankruptcy legislation in 1801. Morris lived the rest of his years on a modest annuity secured by his wife from their old friend and business partner, Gouverneur Morris. But despite his personal decline in fortune, Robert Morris had contributed richly to the founding of a nation that would go on to attain extraordinary wealth and prosperity.

BELOW: *A painting by Jean Leon Gerome Ferris depicts Betsy Ross showing Major George Ross (her husband's uncle) and Robert Morris how she cut the stars for the American flag. George Washington is seated at left.*

Robert Livingston

1746—1813

It has long been a tradition for the chief justice of the Supreme Court to administer the oath of office to the president. But when George Washington was sworn in as the first president of the United States, the Supreme Court had not yet been formed. So the honor of swearing in the president went to the highest-ranking judicial official in New York State (New York City was then the new nation's capital), Chancellor Robert Livingston.

Robert Livingston was born to a wealthy and influential family in New York City in 1746. The Livingstons could trace a direct lineage to British aristocracy, specifically to the Earl of Livingstone in Scotland. At the age of fifteen, Livingston began attending King's College (now Columbia University), studying law before starting a practice with a fellow classmate, John Jay (who later became a relative through marriage). His great skill and success as a lawyer garnered Livingston an appointment to a city judicial post by New York's governor, but his dedication to the independence movement led to his dismissal.

In 1775, Livingston was elected to represent New York at the Continental Congress. He called for delaying the move toward independence—in part, perhaps, because New York's provincial congress had not authorized him to go that far. Then, probably in an effort to prod New York's officials, Livingston was appointed to the committee (including Thomas Jefferson, Benjamin Franklin, John Adams, and Roger Sherman) whose task was to draft the Declaration of Independence, although he does not appear to have played any significant role in its drafting or final version. In any case, Livingston did not sign the Declaration because he had been called back to New York to help frame the state's constitution, which was adopted on April 20, 1777. During the Revolution, Livingston lent an expertise in financial matters toward supplying colonial troops.

In 1781, under the Articles of Confederation, Livingston served as the new nation's first secretary of foreign affairs, equivalent to the secretary of state under the Constitution. Livingston served in the position for less than two years, but showed himself to be an effective diplomat. He was also elected

BELOW: A Currier and Ives lithograph of George Washington's inauguration on April 30, 1789. Robert Livingston administers the oath of office while Samuel Otis holds the Bible borrowed from a Masonic temple.

chancellor, or presiding judge, of the New York Chancery, a position he would come to be closely associated with, retaining it for some twenty-four years. After the United States Constitution was signed in 1787, Livingston supported and advocated for its ratification in New York.

On April 30, 1789, George Washington arrived at Federal Hall in New York City, prepared to take the presidential oath of office. Livingston borrowed a Bible for the ceremony from the nearby Masonic temple where he was a high-ranking member. The inauguration took place on the balcony before an assembled crowd of representatives, senators, and citizens. The simple thirty-five-word oath, as proscribed by the Constitution, was administered by Livingston, who then turned to the crowd and exclaimed, "Long live George Washington, president of the United States!"

Livingston continued on as chancellor of New York until 1801 when he was required by constitutional provision to give up the post. Meanwhile, Livingston had fallen out with his former Federalist colleagues—including Washington, Jay, and Hamilton—over both personal and political issues and had gone over to Jefferson's Democrat-Republican party. So it was that in 1801 he accepted an appointment as minister to France by then President Jefferson. Livingston's diplomatic abilities were well received in France by Emperor Napoleon Bonaparte, who admired Livingston's self-confident, forthright manner. In 1803, Livingston was instrumental in negotiating the purchase of the Louisiana Territory from France. Along with James Madison, Livingston struck a deal for the territory that roughly doubled the area of the United States for the purchase price of fifteen million dollars.

Letter to the Peace Commissioners
March 25, 1782

But, gentlemen, though the issue of your treaty has been successful. though I am satisfied that we are much indebted to your firmness and perseverance, to your accurate knowledge of our situation and of our wants for this success, yet I feel no little pain at the distrust manifested in the management of it; particularly in the signing the treaty without communicating it to the court of Versailles until after the signature, and in concealing the separate article from it even when signed. I have examined, with the most minute attention, all the reasons assigned in your several letters to justify these suspicions. I confess they do not appear to strike me so forcibly as they have done you; and it gives me pain that the character for candor and fidelity to its engagements which should always characterize a great people should have been impeached thereby. The concealment was, in my opinion, absolutely unnecessary....

In declaring my sentiments freely, I invite you to treat me with equal candor in your letters....Upon the whole, I have the pleasure of assuring you that the services you have rendered your country in bringing this business to a happy issue, are very gratefully received by them, however we ay differ in sentiments about the mode of doing it....

ABOVE: Robert Fulton (left) and Napoleon Bonaparte discuss Fulton's steamship invention. While in France, Robert Livingston struck up a partnership with Fulton to bring the steamship to America.

While in France, Livingston was intrigued by the work of a brilliant young American engineer, Robert Fulton. Livingston and Fulton shared a fascination for steam engines and worked together to build a practical steamboat. After successful tests on the Seine, Livingston and Fulton returned to U.S. soil to try to build steamboats that could navigate up the rivers of the United States. In 1807, the two constructed a steamship that managed the voyage up the Hudson from New York to Albany, averaging a record five miles per hour against the current. This ship, the *Clermont*, named after Livingston's estate, was the first practical steamship in the world. Livingston and Fulton set up a river shipping company with a fleet of steamships, one even bearing the name the *Chancellor Livingston*.

When Livingston retired from public life, it was by no means an idle retirement. He continued developing farm techniques, using his estate as a showcase for his ideas on fertilization and introducing several fruit trees to the United States, as well as being one of the first to bring merino sheep to the farming communities west of the Hudson. Livingston died at his estate in 1813 at the age of sixty-seven. His dedicated service to his country, gentlemanly demeanor, and eloquent style was characterized by Benjamin Franklin, who called Livingston the "Cicero of America."

PART THREE

Founding a Nation

(1784—1788)

It was January 14, 1784, before the Congress had a copy of the Treaty of Paris and was able to ratify it. This meant that the new United States of America was not only freed from conducting a costly war with Great Britain, but that it was completely free to govern itself under the Articles of Confederation that had been adopted in 1781. It might have seemed that the new nation was fully "founded," but in fact there remained much work to be done.

Some of it was the ordinary business of starting up a new nation. Disagreements about boundaries between the states had to be negotiated, decisions had to be taken over the disposition of the vast and unknown lands to the west, treaties with the Native Americans had to be arranged, ambassadors had to be appointed—John Adams was named ambassador to Britain, for example, and Thomas Jefferson would be named ambassador to France. Then there were issues with foreign powers—the British who refused to vacate their forts in the Great Lakes region, the Barbary pirates off the north coast of Africa who continued to harass shipping, the Spanish who were determined to retain control of the Mississippi River.

But underneath all these matters was the growing sense that the Articles of Confederation were simply not working to hold these thirteen states together. It was too loose, too indecisive. And there was still not a sense of a loyalty to a central government, still not a sense of individual states setting aside their own wishes and wants for the good of a nation. Many of their disputes centered around interstate commerce and taxes and related financial issues. In February 1786, for example, New Jersey's legislature voted flatly to refuse to send the funds required by the Congress.

So it was that, at the suggestion of the state of Virginia, states were asked to send delegates to attend a conference in Annapolis, Maryland, that September to work out some of these differences. When only five states sent delegates, it was agreed that a meeting should be held in Philadelphia in May 1787, this one

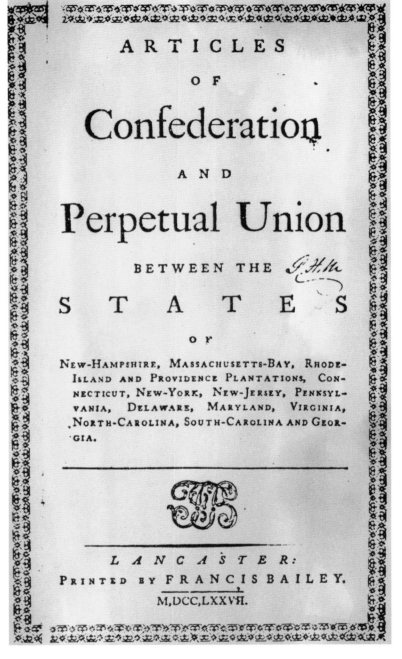

ARTICLES

OF

Confederation

AND

Perpetual Union

BETWEEN THE

STATES

OF

NEW-HAMPSHIRE, MASSACHUSETTS-BAY, RHODE-ISLAND AND PROVIDENCE PLANTATIONS, CONNECTICUT, NEW-YORK, NEW-JERSEY, PENNSYLVANIA, DELAWARE, MARYLAND, VIRGINIA, NORTH-CAROLINA, SOUTH-CAROLINA AND GEORGIA.

LANCASTER:

PRINTED BY FRANCIS BAILEY.

M,DCC,LXXVII.

PREVIOUS PAGE: The Foundation of American Government, by artist Henry Hintermeister, features George Washington and Benjamin Franklin at the signing of the United States Constitution.

LEFT: *The title page for the first printed copy of the Articles of Confederation, initially agreed upon by Congress in 1777 and finally adopted in 1781. The Articles of Confederation was the law of the land in the United States for seven years.*

BELOW: *George Washington presides as president of the Constitutional Convention in Philadelphia in 1787 in a painting by American artist Junius Brutus Stearns.*

to deal with what were now recognized as major political issues that went beyond merely commercial disagreements. Still the original conception was simply that the delegates would revise the Articles of Confederation.

If the solid citizens of the thirteen states required any further reminder that their government needed strengthening, however, it came in August 1786, when hundreds of disgruntled men in Massachusetts—many led by a former Revolutionary War officer, Daniel Shays—mounted what was basically an insurgency to protest mortgage foreclosures and other perceived inequities. By the time this was put down in February 1787, only a few men had been killed, but the very thought of other such uprisings only confirmed the need in the minds of the many Americans that the government needed to be strengthened.

The delegates who gathered in Philadelphia beginning on May 14, 1787, included many of the most distinguished leaders from the thirteen states.

The Constitution of the United States of America
1787

We the People of the United States, in Order to form a more perfect Union, establish Justice, insure domestic Tranquility, provide for the common defence, promote the general Welfare, and secure the Blessings of Liberty to ourselves and our Posterity, do ordain and establish this Constitution for the United States of America.

ARTICLE I

Section 1. All legislative Powers herein granted shall be vested in a Congress of the United States, which shall consist of a Senate and House of Representatives.

Section 2. The House of Representatives shall be composed of Members chosen every second Year by the People of the several States, and the Electors in each State shall have the Qualifications requisite for Electors of the most numerous Branch of the State Legislature....

Representatives and direct Taxes shall be apportioned among the several States which may be included within this Union, according to their respective Numbers, which shall be determined by adding to the whole Number of free Persons, including those bound to Service for a Term of Years, and excluding Indians not taxed, three fifths of all other Persons.....

Section 3. The Senate of the United States shall be composed of two Senators from each State, chosen by the Legislature thereof, for six Years; and each Senator shall have one Vote....

ARTICLE II

Section 1. The executive Power shall be vested in a President of the United States of America. He shall hold his Office during the Term of four Years, and, together with the Vice President, chosen for the same Term,...

ARTICLE III

Section 1. The judicial Power of the United States, shall be vested in one supreme Court, and in such inferior Courts as the Congress may from time to time ordain and establish.

The Judges, both of the supreme and inferior Courts, shall hold their Offices during good Behaviour, and shall, at stated Times, receive for their Services, a Compensation, which shall not be diminished during their Continuance in Office.

ARTICLE VII

The Ratification of the Conventions of nine States, shall be sufficient for the Establishment of this Constitution between the States so ratifying the Same. Done in Convention by the Unanimous Consent of the States present the Seventeenth Day of September in the Year of our Lord one thousand seven hundred and Eighty seven and of the Independence of the United States of America the Twelfth In witness whereof We have hereunto subscribed our Names,

George Washington—President and deputy from Virginia

NEW HAMPSHIRE: John Langdon, Nicholas Gilman

MASSACHUSETTS: Nathaniel Gorham, Rufus King

CONNECTICUT: William Samuel Johnson, Roger Sherman

NEW YORK: Alexander Hamilton

NEW JERSEY: William Livingston, David Brearly, William Paterson, Jonathan Dayton

PENNSYLVANIA: Benjamin Franklin, Thomas Mifflin, Robert Morris, George Clymer, Thomas FitzSimons, Jared Ingersoll, James Wilson, Gouverneur Morris

DELAWARE: George Read, Gunning Bedford, Jr., John Dickinson, Richard Bassett, Jacob Broom

MARYLAND: James McHenry, Daniel of Saint Thomas Jenifer, Daniel Carroll

VIRGINIA: John Blair, James Madison, Jr.

NORTH CAROLINA: William Blount, Richard Dobbs Spaight, Hugh Williamson

SOUTH CAROLINA: John Rutledge, Charles Cotesworth Pinckney, Charles Pinckney, Pierce Butler

GEORGIA: William Few, Abraham Baldwin

The LOOKING GLASS for 1787

CONNECTICUT

New York

From Connecticut to New York having L4000 per annum Impost.

ABOVE: *A political cartoon from 1787 illustrates the struggle between Federalists and Anti-Federalists. Connecticut, represented by a wagon mired in the mud, is pulled by opposing factions. An Anti-Federalist, pulling towards flames and dark clouds, declares, "Success to Shays," an allusion to Shays's Rebellion.*

(In fact, Rhode Island did not send any delegates because it did not want any further governmental role in its affairs.) Benjamin Franklin was among the most respected but at eighty-one years old he was regarded as too old to take on the leadership and George Washington was named president. Knowing that there were going to be long and serious debates, there had to be floor managers, and among these were such men as James Madison, George Mason, Gouverneur Morris, Roger Sherman, and James Wilson. Of these, James Madison would emerge as arguably the most influential because he worked so hard to bring about the necessary compromises.

The first plan debated was the Virginia Plan presented by Edmund Randolph; its distinguishing feature was that there would be two houses in the legislature, with the delegates in both proportional to each state's population. Inevitably, this was resisted by the smaller states, and they supported a plan submitted by New Jersey that called for an equal number of representatives in both houses. It was not until July that Connecticut presented a compromise: an upper house with two senators from each state and the lower house with representatives based on population. With that decided, the many other aspects of the new government were debated.

Among the most troubling issues was that of slavery, and here again, a compromise was reached: the foreign trade in slaves would cease in 1808, while only three-fifths of the population of slaves would be counted among a state's total population for purposes of assigning members to the House of Representatives. Underlying many of the debates were two issues: just how much power should be given to the majority of the people as opposed to being vested in an elite minority, and just how much authority was to be vested in the central government as opposed to being reserved for the individual states.

Finally in September, Gouverneur Morris from New York was delegated to write out a final draft that incorporated all the many terms and decisions previously agreed to, and on September 17, 1787, thirty-nine of the delegates voted to adopt it and signed it. But now it had to be accepted by nine of the thirteen states. And the issue that had come to divide the delegates at the Constitutional Convention spilled out into the open among the citizens of the various states. In general, it was the somewhat more urban, more commercially oriented states of the North who called for a stronger central government. Their leading spokesmen would become known as the Federalists. Meanwhile it was the more rural, agriculturally oriented states of the South that wanted to reserve more powers for individual states.

ABOVE: *The first of four pages comprising the United States Constitution. Adopted and signed on September 17, 1787, the Constitution officially went into effect on June 21, 1788, when New Hampshire's ratification fulfilled the two-thirds requirement.*

RIGHT TOP: *A 1799 print of The Federalist, a collection of essays by Alexander Hamilton, James Madison, and John Jay, arguing in favor of a strong central government embodied in the United States Constitution.*

RIGHT BOTTOM: *A cartoon published in a 1788 edition of the Massachusetts Centinel, just after New York became the eleventh state to ratify the U.S. Constitution.*

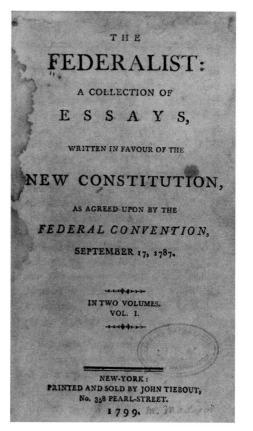

What ensued for the next few months was a major national debate, conducted mainly through newspaper articles, pamphlets, and debates at each state's ratifying conventions. The most eloquent and profound of the supporting arguments appeared in a series of eighty-five essays composed by Alexander Hamilton, James Madison, and John Jay. Seventy-seven of these first appeared as letters in a New York newspaper, the *Independent Journal* before all eighty-five were published in a book titled *The Federalist*. But even some of the staunchest supporters of the new nation—men like Richard Henry Lee, Patrick Henry, George Mason, and Edmund Randolph—spoke out against adopting the Constitution. On the other side, men like James Wilson and Roger Sherman lent their voices in support.

On December 7, 1787, Delaware became the first state to ratify the Constitution and on June 21, 1788, New Hampshire became the ninth, so technically the Constitution was the law of the land. But until the two powerful states of Virginia and New York ratified it, the situation remained perilous; finally Virginia did so on June 25, 1788, and New York followed on July 26, 1788. North Carolina and Rhode Island continued to hold off ratifying until they were promised a bill of rights, but they did participate in the national elections that ensued. The work of the Founding Fathers was not yet completed.

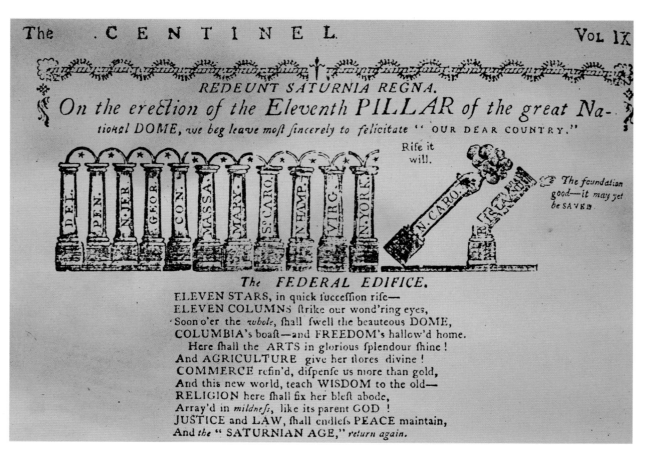

James Madison

1751—1836

Opposite: A portrait of America's fourth president, James Madison, by artist Thomas Sully. Madison has been called the father of both the Constitution and the Bill of Rights.

Below: A list of approximately 1,300 books that James Madison submitted to Congress in 1783, which he felt should be made available to members of Congress. The proposal was the basis for what would eventually become the Library of Congress.

Among the Founding Fathers, James Madison alone has been known as the father of two of the most seminal documents that have served as the foundation of American society: the Constitution and the Bill of Rights. That was consistent with a career of a man who juggled many issues.

The son of a Virginia planter with 4,000 acres of land and about a hundred slaves, young James spent five years at a boarding school and two years of tutoring at home, before speeding through the College of New Jersey (later renamed Princeton University) in two years. Sleeping no more than five hours a night in college, he was influenced by thinkers like John

Federalist Paper No. 51: The Structure of the Government Must Furnish the Proper Checks and Balances Between the Different Departments
February 6, 1788

To the People of the State of New York:

TO WHAT expedient, then, shall we finally resort, for maintaining in practice the necessary partition of power among the several departments, as laid down in the Constitution? The only answer that can be given is, that as all these exterior provisions are found to be inadequate, the defect must be supplied, by so contriving the interior structure of the government as that its several constituent parts may, by their mutual relations, be the means of keeping each other in their proper places. Without presuming to undertake a full development of this important idea, I will hazard a few general observations, which may perhaps place it in a clearer light, and enable us to form a more correct judgment of the principles and structure of the government planned by the convention.

In order to lay a due foundation for that separate and distinct exercise of the different powers of government, which to a certain extent is admitted on all hands to be essential to the preservation of liberty, it is evident that each department should have a will of its own; and consequently should be so constituted that the members of each should have as little agency as possible in the appointment of the members of the others. Were this principle rigorously adhered to, it would require that all the appointments for the supreme executive, legislative, and judiciary magistracies should be drawn from the same fountain of authority, the people, through channels having no communication whatever with one another. Perhaps such a plan of constructing the several departments would be less difficult in practice than it may in contemplation appear. Some difficulties, however, and some additional expense would attend the execution of it. Some deviations, therefore, from the principle must be admitted. In the constitution of the judiciary department in particular, it might be inexpedient to insist rigorously on the principle:

first, because peculiar qualifications being essential in the members, the primary consideration ought to be to select that mode of choice which best secures these qualifications; secondly, because the permanent tenure by which the appointments are held in that department, must soon destroy all sense of dependence on the authority conferring them.

It is equally evident, that the members of each department should be as little dependent as possible on those of the others, for the emoluments annexed to their offices. Were the executive magistrate, or the judges, not independent of the legislature in this particular, their independence in every other would be merely nominal.

But the great security against a gradual concentration of the several powers in the same department, consists in giving to those who administer each department the necessary constitutional means and personal motives to resist encroachments of the others. The provision for defense must in this, as in all other cases, be made commensurate to the danger of attack. Ambition must be made to counteract ambition. The interest of the man must be connected with the constitutional rights of the place. It may be a reflection on human nature, that such devices should be necessary to control the abuses of government. But what is government itself, but the greatest of all reflections on human nature? If men were angels, no government would be necessary. If angels were to govern men, neither external nor internal controls on government would be necessary. In framing a government which is to be administered by men over men, the great difficulty lies in this: you must first enable the government to control the governed; and in the next place oblige it to control itself. A dependence on the people is, no doubt, the primary control on the government; but experience has taught mankind the necessity of auxiliary precautions....

ABOVE: *An arcane political cartoon critical of the American position in the War of 1812 by British artist, George Cruikshank. Opposing Britannia, James Madison stands dismayed between the devil and Napoleon, who was also at war with Britain. Cruikshank is well-known for his illustrations of Charles Dickens's novels.*

Locke and Isaac Newton, but also by political activists at one of the country's most progressive institutions. Madison's overwork caused him to suffer debilitating health problems that kept him from military service, but he plunged into politics upon graduation.

After returning home, he joined his father on the Orange County Committee of Safety, under what he called "very early and strong impressions in favor of liberty both civil and religious." Two year later, he served in the Virginia Convention that championed independence and a state constitution. In the debate over this constitution, he successfully petitioned to alter a religious-toleration clause into one guaranteeing "liberty of conscience for all."

Serving in the Continental Congress (1779–1783) as an advocate of strong central government, he was known as its most effective and informed member. He returned to the Virginia House of Delegates (1784–86), which under his leadership called for a national convention of states. The Annapolis Convention he attended in 1786 so splintered over a proposed treaty with Spain and federal commerce power that it threatened to break up the country into regional federations. Madison saw local interests fracturing the good of the union. The following year, he was sent to Philadelphia's historic Constitutional Convention.

He argued persuasively for a chief executive, a bicameral legislature, and an independent judiciary balancing the interests of states governing local affairs.

LEFT: *Dolley Madison was one of America's most popular first ladies. During the War of 1812, while fleeing British soldiers advancing on the White House, Dolley famously saved a Gilbert Stuart portrait of George Washington.*

A central government could not function effectively if it was subordinated to the states, he argued, supporting the Virginia Plan and opposing the weak-federation New Jersey Plan. The Connecticut Compromise that emerged from Philadelphia differed from some of his ideas, but he was generally recognized to be the most important framer and it is his notes on the proceedings that have provided history with the best sense of what went on at the convention.

At the Virginia Convention called to ratify the Constitution—the state was the most populous and influential in the union—Madison outdebated states' rights advocate Patrick Henry and won ratification. With Alexander Hamilton and John Jay, Madison also produced the *Federalist Papers*, urging all states to ratify the Constitution. Madison's essays particularly stressed the need to accept the compromises embodied in the constitution and the importance of the "checks and balances" that would govern the actions of the three branches of the new government.

RIGHT: *A cartoon by American artist Charles William reveling in an American naval victory over Britain in the War of 1812. King George III is bloodied by James Madison, whose dialogue refers to the victory of the American frigate* Enterprise *over the* Boxer *in September 1813.*

There was yet another important document in his future. Madison was concerned that a strong central government could erode individual rights. Therefore, upon election to the country's initial House of Representatives, he drafted the first ten amendments to the Constitution: the Bill of Rights.

He remained in Congress until 1797, detouring from his busy schedule in 1794 to marry a lively widow named Dolley Payne Todd, who became one of history's most engaging hostesses. By this time, Madison was coming to fear that the limited government he favored was swelling into a monolith favoring wealthy commercial interests. Madison's concern for individuals thus led him away from the strong-government Federalists of the George Washington and John Adams presidencies into the emerging Democratic-Republican (later Democratic) party. After leaving Congress, he drafted the Virginia Resolutions against Adams's short-lived Alien and Sedition Acts, which among other things equated press criticism of the president with treason.

As Thomas Jefferson's secretary of state (1801–09), Madison helped double the size of the country with the Louisiana Purchase in 1803. Although he argued that neutral countries should be able to trade with warring powers, he had to support Jefferson's Embargo Act, which kept all ships in their ports while forbidding exports and succeeded only in hurting U.S. trade.

In 1808, Madison was elected the country's fourth president, defeating Federalist Charles C. Pinckney 122-47 in the electoral college. Madison's mechanical rather than charismatic style served him poorly during eight years as chief executive. In 1809, Congress replaced the Embargo Act with the equally ineffective Non-Intercourse Act, which allowed trade with all nations except Great Britain and France. Both countries continued to raid American ships and impress seamen, so in 1810 Congress tried a different approach. It passed an act stating that the United States would trade only with the country that ceased raiding American ships. France agreed to stop these practices—a false promise in the end—and meantime the British were accused of stirring up Indians in the western territories of the United States. Realizing that many Americans were now furious at the British, in June 1812 Madison convinced Congress to declare war against Britain. Refusing to change leaders amid hostilities, the American people re-elected Madison, who defeated Federalist DeWitt Clinton, 128-89.

With only fourteen warships, fewer than 7,000 trained soldiers, a crippled treasury, and a nation so divided that New England refused to arm its men (and would come close to threatening to secede), the United States was ill-equipped to fight the British. During thirty months of war, Americans saw Washington, D.C., sacked and the White House burned. Madison watched the inferno from across the Potomac River, where he and Dolley had fled and where she had spirited some presidential papers and Gilbert Stuart's

ABOVE: Impressment of American Seamen, *a painting by Howard Pyle, showing British sailors seizing American seamen for the Royal Navy. The practice added to tensions between the nations leading up to the War of 1812.*

portrait of George Washington. Nonetheless, the union held together after critical victories in Baltimore and on Lake Champlain. The war ended strangely in December of 1814. With peace representatives sent to Ghent (now in Belgium) but not heard from, a large British force was approaching Louisiana by sea. New Englander Federalists from the Hartford Convention were converging on Washington demanding to be heard. All at once, news of a treaty arrived from Europe and of a spectacular U.S. victory from the Battle of New Orleans. Amid the celebration, the Federalist Party began a rapid collapse, its cries of "Mr. Madison's war" suddenly meaningless.

Following the war, Madison capitalized on national optimism by getting Congress to create roads, canals and a new national bank, while taxing imports. After leaving office, he succeeded his friend Jefferson as president of the University of Virginia and developed scientific farming methods widely adopted a century later. The last surviving Founding Father, Madison died at his Montpelier, Virginia, estate on June 28, 1836. His final words for Americans: "The advice nearest to my heart and deepest in my convictions is that the Union of the States be cherished and perpetuated."

ABOVE: *A British cartoon mocking President James Madison and presumably his secretary of war, John Armstrong, shown fleeing Washington, D.C., during the War of 1812. The fire set by British soldiers that consumed the White House is visible in the background.*

RIGHT: *A British wood engraving depicting the burning of Washington, D.C., by British forces during the War of 1812. The text at the bottom lists the structures torched in the attack, including the "Senate House, Presidents Palace, War Office, [and] Treasury."*

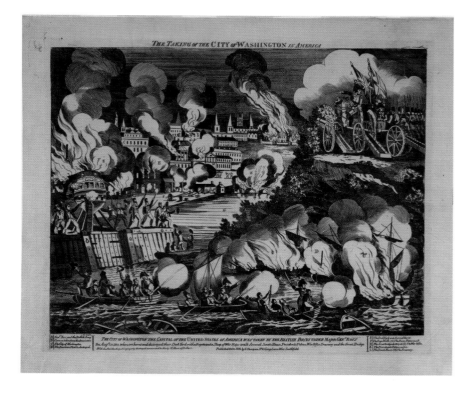

Gouverneur Morris

1752—1816

Born into a wealthy New York family, Gouverneur Morris experienced a life that was not without setbacks. When young, his arm was badly scalded and disfigured; he later lost a leg in a carriage accident. His disabilities did not prevent him from engaging in a vigorous public life, and he exercised great influence in politics and commerce.

He graduated from King's College (later Columbia University) at the age of sixteen in 1768. After three years of reading law, he was admitted to the bar. During New York's first flush of patriotic fervor in the 1770s, the young Morris remained an agnostic. His conservative upbringing had cultivated in him a distrust of too much democracy.

Morris's thinking began to shift when he encountered patriots, such as John Jay and Alexander Hamilton, also graduates of King's College. As relations with Britain deteriorated, Morris took a seat in New York's provincial congress of 1775, where he advocated resistance. Although exempt from the military because of his handicaps, and also because he held public office, Morris joined a militia company. By early 1776 he was asked to serve as second in command of a regiment, but neither the regiment nor he saw action.

Morris turned his attention to legislation, drafting the New York state constitution in 1777, but the British soon invaded New York City and its environs. Morris's mother, a loyalist, offered the British use of the family estate, effectively making Morris a war refugee. Fleeing to Pennsylvania,

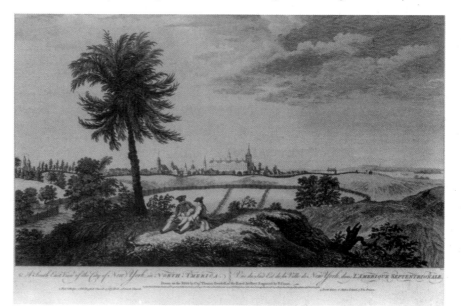

Letter to George Washington
Philadelphia, October 30, 1787

Dear Sir,

Shortly after your departure from this place, I went to my farm, and returned hither last Sunday evening. Living out of the busy world, I had nothing to say worth your attention, or I should earlier have given you the trouble you must now experience. Although not very inquisitive about political opinion, I have not been quite inattentive. The States eastward of New York appear to be almost unanimous in favor of the new Constitution (for I make no account of the dissension in Rhode Island)...

Jersey is so near unanimity in her favorable opinion, that we may count with certainty on something more than votes, should the state of affairs hereafter require the application of pointed arguments. New York, hemmed in between the war friends of the Constitution, will not easily, unless supported by powerful States, make any important struggle, even though her citizens were unanimous, which is by no means the case...

With respect to this State [Pennsylvania], I am far from being decided in my opinion, that they will consent... What opinions prevail more southward I cannot guess. You are in a better condition, than any other person, to judge of a great and important part of that country.

I have observed that your name to the new Constitution has been of infinite service. Indeed, I am convinced that if you had not attended the Convention, and the same paper had been handed out to the world, it would have met with a colder reception, with fewer and weaker advocates, and with more and more strenuous opponents. As it is, should the idea prevail that you will not accept of the presidency, it would prove fatal in many parts. The truth is, that your great and decided superiority leads men willingly to put you in a place, which will not add to your personal dignity, nor raise you higher than you already stand. But they would not readily put any other person in the same situation, because they feel the elevation of others, as operating by comparison the degradation of themselves, and, however absurd this idea may be, yet you will agree with me, that men must be treated as men, and not as machines, much less as philosophers, and least of all things as reasonable creatures, seeing that in effect they reason, not to direct but to excuse, their conduct.

Thus much for the public opinion on these subjects, which is not to be neglected in a country where opinion is everything.

Morris joined the Continental Congress there in 1777; during this time he wrote *Observations on the American Revolution*. Published by Congress, the pamphlet praised the American nation as a haven of freedom.

As a member of a congressional committee, Morris visited Washington's winter encampment in Valley Forge, where he was appalled by the "army of skeletons." Thereafter, he emerged as a congressional ally of the Continental army. He signed the Articles of Confederation, instructed Benjamin Franklin on his diplomatic missions to Paris, and contributed to the treaty ending the Revolution.

Filled with a sense of his self-worth, Morris spoke frankly, even caustically, so much so that he alienated many colleagues. He supported a strong central government, which most New Yorkers opposed, and in 1779 Morris was defeated for re-election. He relocated to Philadelphia where he practiced law.

In 1781, he reentered public service as an assistant to the minister of finance, a department akin to the Treasury. In 1782 Morris urged decimalization (coining the word "cent"). He also sought to persuade former loyalists, his mother included, to support the nation. At the same time, he critiqued the nation's jerry-rigged governing and financial institutions, as in his *Address on the Abolition of the Bank of North America* (1785).

In 1787, he served as a member of the Pennsylvania delegation to the Constitutional Convention at Philadelphia, where he emerged as a leading voice. He argued for religious liberty, spoke in opposition to slavery, and defended the right of property and the rule of law. In all, he spoke 173 times, more than any other delegate. A nationalist who advocated union over confederation, Morris drafted extensive sections of the Constitution, including its preamble with its famous opening, "We the People of the United States, in order to form a more perfect Union...." As one of his letters to George Washington reveals, Morris was well aware of the resistance of even his fellow Pennsylvanians to a strong federal government, but in the end Pennsylvania ratified the Constitution.

In 1788, Morris sailed to France to engage in land speculation and other ventures. He undertook a diplomatic mission to London in 1790, conducting negotiations between Britain and France. Washington appointed Morris minister to France in 1792, where he served during the French Revolution.

BELOW: *An illustration by British artist Isaac Cruikshank, critical of French revolutionaries. A sansculotte is pictured wearing a belt reading, "War Eternal War." Gouverneur Morris was also critical of revolutionaries while serving as minister to France, siding with royalists.*

A REPUBLICAN BEAU.
A Picture of Paris for 1794

Morris's sympathies were with the royalists, however, and he was recalled in 1794. What Morris saw of the Reign of Terror strengthened his resolve to oppose abuses of authority. When he returned home in 1799, the political atmosphere had changed and his opinions were those of a minority.

Jefferson and the Democratic-Republicans swept John Adams from the presidency in 1800, but Morris, running as a Federalist, won election to finish an unexpired term in the Senate. His unrelenting criticism of Jefferson and lack of a politician's popular touch caused his defeat in 1802. Retiring from politics, Morris enjoyed a robust social life. He served from 1810 to 1813 as chairman of the Erie Canal Commission. In 1816, he died at his estate in New York.

An eyewitness to two revolutions, a key constitutional framer, an irascible Federalist, Gouverneur Morris shaped a political and social order at odds with the world into which he had been born. Yet he remained devoted to the ideal of the union, to the definition of himself not as a citizen of a state but as a citizen of a nation. In the words of Theodore Roosevelt, Morris was "emphatically an American first."

Roger Sherman

1721–1793

The Constitutional Convention had reached an impasse over the issue of the number of representatives in a new national legislature. Smaller states wanted there to be equal representation from all the states. The larger states wanted representation to be apportioned based on population size. Without some form of agreement between the two sides, there would be no United States of America. A compromise had to be reached. The solution came in part from a former shoe cobbler from Connecticut, Roger Sherman.

Sherman was born in Newton, Massachusetts, of humble origins. The son of a cobbler, Sherman followed naturally in his father's footsteps in learning the trade. Although he had little formal schooling, the young cobbler possessed an insatiable curiosity and a thirst for knowledge that drove him to begin a self-education that would last his entire life. Upon his father's death in 1743, Sherman moved to New Milford, Connecticut, where he began branching out into new areas of interest, including the study of law. Sherman was admitted to the bar in 1754, working as counselor, justice of the peace, and judge, and was eventually elected to represent New Milford in the Connecticut Assembly. In 1761, drawn to the scholarship of Yale College, Sherman relocated to New Haven, Connecticut. At Yale, he served as treasurer and was eventually bestowed an honorary master's degree from the prestigious institution.

In 1774 and again in 1775, Sherman served as representative of Connecticut at the Continental Congress. As a measure of the high esteem in which he was held by members of the Second Continental Congress, Sherman was appointed to serve alongside John Adams, Thomas Jefferson, Benjamin Franklin, and Robert R. Livingston, as one of the Committee of Five, charged with drafting the Declaration of Independence. As one of four representatives of Connecticut, Sherman signed his name to the Declaration on August 2, 1776.

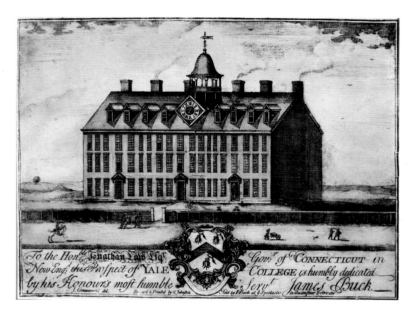

ABOVE: *An illustration of Yale College from 1749. The New Haven, Connecticut, school bestowed an honorary master's degree on Roger Sherman in 1768 in recognition of his service and dedication.*

LEFT: *A portrait of Roger Sherman by artist John Ferguson Weir from a miniature by John Trumbull. Sherman holds a quill pen in his hand, signifying his status as one of only two men to sign three of America's major founding documents.*

Mayor Roger Sherman

LEFT: *A sketch by Irving L. Hurlburt of Roger Sherman while mayor of New Haven. Sherman held the post for two years, from 1784 to 1786.*

In 1778, Sherman added his signature to another of the foundation documents, the Articles of Confederation, which he also helped draft. Having worked to craft these two seminal documents, it was only natural that Sherman was enlisted to help negotiate the U.S. Constitution. During the Constitutional Convention, Sherman was very active, serving on various committees and delivering more than a hundred speeches. One of the main sticking points between the delegates at the convention concerned the issue of apportioning representation. The contentious issue of slavery also compounded the disagreement, with southern states wanting to add the slave population to their overall representation totals. Luther Martin of Maryland wrote, "We were on the verge of dissolution, scarce held together by the strength of an hair."

Sherman, along with Oliver Ellsworth, proposed a compromise. The House of Representatives would be elected based on population. The Senate would be composed of two representatives from each state. As to the issue of slave populations, southern states were allowed to count white citizens and three-fifths of "all other persons," the euphemism used in the wording of the Constitution so as not to include the word "slaves" in the document. In order to break the impasse, all had to give up something in what was called the Great Compromise, also

BELOW: *A Currier and Ives lithograph illustrating the committee charged with drafting the Declaration of Independence. From left to right: Thomas Jefferson, Roger Sherman, Benjamin Franklin, John Adams, and Robert R. Livingston.*

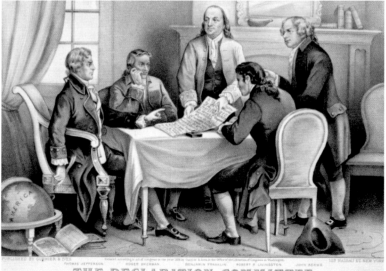

THE DECLARATION COMMITTEE.

There is another thing, in this new constitution, that my neighbour and me, have talked a good deal about; it is what is called in the writings you sent me, [Article I, Section 9, Clause I]. Indeed, we hardly know what they will be at by this; for fear you should mistake me, I believe I had better write it down; they say, "the migration, or importation of such persons, as any of the states now existing shall think proper to admit, shall not be prohibited by the congress, prior to the year 1808, but a tax, or duty may be imposed on such importation, not exceeding ten dollars for each person."

...[O]ur old neighbour from Pennsylvania, says, that it is thought among them...that its true meaning, is to give leave to import negroes from Guinea, for slaves, to work upon the rich men's plantations, to the southward; but that it is not mentioned plainly on purpose, because the quakers, and a great many other good religious people, are very much against making slaves of our fellow-creatures, and especially, against suffering any more to be brought into the country, and this, if it was known, might make them all against the new government: now, if this is really the case, it is to be sure, much worse than my neighbour and me first thought it to be; for all good christians must agree, that this trade is an abomination to the Lord, and must, if continued, bring down a heavy judgment upon our land. It does not seem to be justice, that one man should take another from his own country, and make a slave of him; and yet we are told by this new constitution, that one of its great ends, is to establish justice;... I well remember, that our congress (and I believe, as I mentioned before, that they were honest, good men who meant as they said) when they declared independence, solemnly said, that "all men were created equal; and that they were endowed by their creator with certain unalienable rights; and that among them, are these, life, liberty, and the pursuit of happiness."....

Alas! my good friend, it is a terrible thing to mock the almighty, for how can we expect to merit his favor, or escape his vengeance; if it should appear, that we were not serious in our professions, and that they were mere devices to gratify our pride and ambition, we ought to remember, he sees into the secret recesses of our hearts, and knows what is passing there. It becomes us then to bear testimony against every thing which may be displeasing in his sight, and be careful that we incur not the charge mentioned by the prophet Hosea, "ye have plowed wickedness, ye have reaped iniquity; ye have eaten the fruit of lies, because thou didst trust in thy ways, in the multitude of thy mighty men."

known as the Connecticut Compromise, in recognition of Sherman and his fellow representatives of the state that would later be dubbed "The Constitution State." Sherman himself played a major role in supporting adoption of the new constitution, among other ways by writing a series of letters to the *New Haven Gazette* using the pseudonym, "A Countryman."

Roger Sherman is one of only two men to have signed all three of the founding documents: The Declaration of Independence, the Articles of Confederation, and the U.S. Constitution. After serving for two years as a representative of Connecticut in the House of Representatives, Sherman rose to the Senate, where he served his state until his death in 1793.

Edmund Randolph

1753–1813

As a member of one of the most distinguished old families of colonial Virginia, Edmund Randolph would take an independent course in the founding of a new nation. After studying law at the College of William and Mary, he supported the Revolution—even though his loyalist parents went to England. Edmund served briefly as an aide-de-camp to George Washington, but in 1776 returned to civilian life where, as a delegate to a state convention, he helped to draft the Virginia Declaration of Rights. He was then elected attorney general of Virginia. He was a delegate to the Second Continental Congress (1779–1782)—the one that adopted the Articles of Confederation—and served as governor of Virginia (1786–88). In 1786, he was a delegate to the convention at Annapolis, Maryland, called to revise the Articles of Confederation under which the states had been operating since 1781. When this meeting proved inconclusive, the states agreed to meet the next year in Philadelphia to consider writing a new constitution.

As a citizen of one of the most populous states, Randolph came to Philadelphia in May 1787 committed to seeing that such states had a larger voice in any new government. And it was not just the issue of population: Randolph was essentially an early proponent of what is known to this day as "states' rights." He thus presented what would be known as the Virginia Plan—or Randolph Plan—that called for a single body of Congress with the number of representatives based solely on the population of the states and their tax contribution. Against this plan was one offered by the delegates from New Jersey that proposed a single body in which each state had the same number of representatives. It remained for the delegates from Connecticut to propose the compromise—a House of Representatives based on population, a Senate with two members from each state. Although Randolph did continue to work on many of the details of the Constitution, and actually participated in writing the first draft, he

Left: A portrait of Edmund Randolph by Italian-born American artist Constantino Brumidi, best known for his frescoes that decorate the Capitol rotunda and other important government buildings in Washington, D.C.

Below: A postcard showing the flight of Lord Dunmore, the last Royal Governor of Virginia. Edmund Randolph and his parents followed different paths during the Revolution, with Randolph fighting for independence while his loyalist parents followed Dunmore back to England.

A Letter of His Excellency Edmund Randolph, Esq., on the Federal Constitution, Addressed to the Honorable Speaker of the House of Delegates, Virginia

October 10, 1787

Sir,

The Constitution, which I enclosed to the General Assembly in a late official letter, appears without my signature. This circumstance, although trivial in its own nature, has been rendered rather important, to myself at least, by being misunderstood by some and misrepresented by others. As I disdain to conceal the reasons for withholding my subscription, I have always been, still am, and ever shall be, ready to proclaim them to the world. To the legislature, therefore, by whom I was deputed to the Federal Convention, I beg leave now to address them; affecting no indifference to public opinion, but resolved not to court it by an unmanly sacrifice of my own judgment. As this explanation will involve a summary but general review of our federal situation, you will pardon me, I trust, although I should transgress the usual bounds of a letter.

Before my departure for the Convention, I believed that the Confederation was not so eminently defective as it had been supposed. But after I had entered into a free communication with those who were best informed of the condition and interest of each state; after I had compared the intelligence derived from them with the properties which ought to characterize the government of our Union,—I became persuaded that the Confederation was destitute of every energy which a constitution of the United States ought to possess.

For the objects proposed by its institution were, that it should be a shield against foreign hostility, and a firm resort against domestic commotion; that it should cherish trade, and promote the prosperity of the states under its care. But these are not among the attributes of our present union. Severe experience under the pressure of war, a ruinous weakness manifested since the return of peace, and the contemplation of those dangers which darken the future prospect, have condemned the hope of grandeur and safety under the auspices of the Confederation.....

But now, sir, permit me to declare that, in my humble judgment, the powers by which alone the blessings of a general government can be accomplished, cannot be interwoven in the Confederation without a change in its very essence; or, in other words, that the Confederation must be thrown aside. This is almost demonstrable, from the inefficacy of requisitions, and from the necessity of converting them into acts of authority. My suffrage, as a citizen, is also for additional powers. But to whom shall we commit these acts of authority—these additional powers? To Congress? When I formerly lamented the defects in the jurisdiction of Congress, I had no view to indicate any other opinion, than that the federal head ought not to be so circumscribed; for, free as I am at all times to profess my reverence for that body, and the individuals who compose it, I am yet equally free to make known my aversion to repose such a trust in a tribunal so constituted. My objections are not the visions of theory, but the result of my own observations in America, and of the experience of others abroad....

Copyright, 1876 by Currier & Ives, N.Y.

GEORGE WASHINGTON.   GEN. HENRY KNOX, Sec'y of War.   ALEXANDER HAMILTON Sec'y of the Treasury   THOMAS JEFFERSON, Sec'y of State   EDMUND RANDOLPH, Attorney General

WASHINGTON AND HIS CABINET.

NEW YORK. PUBLISHED BY CURRIER & IVES, 125 NASSAU ST.

ABOVE: *A Currier and Ives lithograph of President George Washington and his cabinet. From left to right: Washington, Secretary of War Henry Knox, Secretary of Treasury Alexander Hamilton, Secretary of State Thomas Jefferson, and Attorney General Edmund Randolph.*

continued to oppose the Connecticut Compromise. He also felt that in general the Constitution was assigning too much power to a central government, and so he refused to sign the adopted document. He felt so strongly that he immediately published a booklet explaining his views, *Letter on the Federal Constitution*.

However, the very next year, when Virginia's legislature met to consider the new Constitution, Randolph revealed his independent streak once more by urging that it be adopted. He was determined to form a new nation and he had decided that it was better for Virginia to play a role in it than to sit on the sidelines. Randolph was rewarded for his position when Washington appointed him as the nation's first attorney general (1789–1793), and he soon became one of Washington's most trusted advisers. Again, too, he revealed an ability to seek compromise by refusing to take sides in the emerging disputes between Alexander Hamilton and Thomas Jefferson and their respective supporters.

Elevated to secretary of state in Washington's second administration, Randolph now tried to maintain neutrality in the increasingly heated national debate between those who favored England and those who favored France in these nations' ongoing war. However, the French ambassador to the United States communicated to his government the suggestion that Randolph might be open to bribery for supporting the French cause. The message was intercepted and although both the ambassador and Randolph would staunchly deny this claim, when Washington confronted Randolph with this charge, he resigned his post in 1795. He returned to Virginia and spent his remaining years practicing law, but so hurt was he by this last experience with Washington—both the man and the government—that he withdrew from the national political stage.

Aside from his participation in several of the formative assemblies of the new nation, Edmund Randolph contributed something arguably far more important to the founding of the United States. Here was this staunch supporter of states' rights who could, in the end, set aside his personal philosophy for the greater good of the new nation. On several occasions, Randolph's actions sent a message that would reverberate in the decades and centuries to come: that the United States of America was often best served not by holding out for a hundred percent, but for practicing what Bismarck described: "Politics is the art of the possible, the attainable...the next best."

James Wilson

1742–1798

Left: *A portrait of James Wilson by artist Albert Rosenthal. The Scottish-born Wilson was known as a fiery orator as well as a profound legal scholar.*

Below: *The State House in Philadelphia (Independence Hall), as it appeared in 1776, where a decade later, James Wilson would advocate for the adoption of the U.S. Constitution. The steeple of the State House was the home of the Liberty Bell for a century, from 1753 to 1852.*

On September 17, 1787, the last day of the Constitutional Convention, James Wilson rose to give one final speech before the delegates, many of who remained unconvinced of the document's worthiness. He had given numerous speeches before the body during the deliberations—the second most of anyone in attendance. But as he rose to speak for the final time, the words that Wilson began to read were not his own. The speech had been penned by Benjamin Franklin, who was too tired to deliver the address himself. Instead he entrusted his words to the orator whom he knew would do them proper justice.

James Wilson was born in Scotland in 1742. He studied at the University of Edinburgh before immigrating to America in 1765. Wilson arrived in Philadelphia where he found the colonists enraged over the recently imposed Stamp Act, and immediately immersed himself in the struggles of his adopted land. He began teaching Latin at the College of

INDEPENDENCE HALL IN 1776

ABOVE: *A procession entering the University of Pennsylvania to hear Supreme Court Justice James Wilson speak. Wilson founded the university's law school in 1790, one of the nation's earliest law schools.*

Philadelphia while also studying law under John Dickinson. After only a year of study, Wilson started his own law practice. In 1774, firmly planting his support behind the independence movement, Wilson wrote a pamphlet called *Considerations on the Nature and Extent of the Legislative Authority of the British Parliament*. It was one of the earliest arguments against Parliament's authority to pass laws over the colonies. On the strength of his words and commitment, Wilson was elected to represent Pennsylvania in the Continental Congress where he added his signature to the Declaration of Independence.

During the Revolution, Wilson continued to serve in the Continental Congress, where he sat on committees that dealt with military and Indian affairs. In 1781, Congress appointed Wilson as director of the Bank of North America, which helped finance the Revolution. With his many abilities and broad knowledge, Wilson was a natural selection to represent Pennsylvania at the Constitutional Convention of 1787.

As a very active member of the convention, Wilson sat on the Committee of Details, which drew up the first draft of the Constitution. He also put his renowned skill as an orator to good use, delivering more speeches than anyone at the convention, save for Gouverneur Morris. On the final day of the convention, Wilson rose to deliver the words entrusted to him by fellow Pennsylvanian, Benjamin Franklin, saying, "On the whole, Sir, I can not help expressing a wish that every member of the convention who may still have objects to it, would with me, on this occasion doubt a little of his own infallibility, and make manifest our unanimity, put his name to this instrument."

As a call for unity, the speech was a success—the Constitution was signed. But ratification of the document still remained. Wilson was again called upon to use his powers of oration to convince Pennsylvanians to accept the new federal system. On October 6, 1787, Wilson spoke of the new

Constitution in the Pennsylvania State House Yard. "[W]hen I reflect how widely men differ in their opinions, and that every man (and observation applies likewise to every State) has an equal pretension to assert his own, I am satisfied that anything nearer to perfection could not have been accomplished....Regarding it then, in every point of view, with a candid and disinterested mind, I am bold to assert, that it is the best form of government which has been offered in to the world."

In 1789, Wilson joined the new national government as an associate justice of the Supreme Court. But despite his earlier glories of oration and intellect, Wilson failed to distinguish himself on the high court. He also experienced numerous failures in land speculation, enough to earn him several short stays in debtors' prison (while still serving as a justice). Wilson died penniless at the age of fifty-six.

Considerations on the Power to Incorporate the Bank of North America
1785

Though the United States in Congress assembled derive from the particular states no power, jurisdiction, or right, which is not expressly delegated by the confederation, it does not thence follow, that the United States in congress have no other powers, jurisdiction, or rights, than those delegated by the particular states. The United States have general rights, general powers, and general obligations, not derived from any particular states, nor from all the particular states, taken separately; but resulting from the union of the whole: and, therefore, it is provided, in the fifth article of the confederation, "that for the more convenient management of the general interests of the United States, delegates shall be annually appointed to meet in congress."

To many purposes, the United States are to be considered as one undivided, independent nation; and as possessed of all the rights, and powers, and properties, by the law of nations incident to such. Whenever an object occurs, to the direction of which no particular state is competent, the management of it must, of necessity, belong to the United States in congress assembled. There are many objects of this extended nature. The purchase, the sale, the defence, and the government of lands and countries, not within any state, are all included under this description. An institution for circulating paper, and establishing its credit over the whole United States, is naturally ranged in the same class....

It is no new position, that rights may be vested in a political body, which did not previously reside in any or in all the members of that body. They may be derived solely from the union of those members. "The case," says the celebrated Burlamaqui, "is here very near the same as in that of several voices collected together, which, by their union, produce a harmony, that was not to be found separately in each."

A number of unconnected inhabitants are settled on each side of a navigable river; it belongs to none of them; it belongs not to them all, for they have nothing in common: let them unite; the river is the property of the united body.

The arguments drawn from the political associations of individuals into a state will apply, with equal force and propriety, to a number of states united by a confederacy....

PART FOUR
Inventing a Government

(1789–1796)

Although the new Constitution had been in force since July 1788, it was still some months before the United States had a functioning government. And it was January 1789 before all the states had selected the electors who would choose the president and vice president. Not that there was any question as to who that president would be: George Washington was the first choice of all the electors who voted on February 4, 1789. John Adams, the recipient of the second highest total of votes, was chosen to be vice president.

Even then, these men were not formally notified or installed. Rather, in the ensuing weeks, each state's legislature selected its two senators, while representatives were selected by a combination of direct popular vote and legislative appointment. These men gathered in the newly chosen capital, New York City, starting in March, but it was April 6 before the Senate counted the electors' ballots and officially announced that Washington and Adams were the winners. Washington would be inaugurated on the balcony of the Federal Hall in New York on April 30.

At the time that Washington launched the government of the United States of America, there were, in fact, only eleven states. Both North Carolina and Rhode Island had withheld endorsement of the Constitution; it would be November 21, 1789, before North Carolina would ratify, while Rhode Island held off until May 29, 1790. The reason these states refused to accept the original constitution is that both feared that it granted too much power to a central government, and to curb this they had insisted that

PREVIOUS PAGE: *George Washington arrives in Philadelphia for his second inauguration on March 4, 1793, in a painting by American artist Jean Leon Gerome Ferris. Washington's two terms set a precedent that would last until Franklin D. Roosevelt was elected to four consecutive terms.*

BELOW: *An engraving of George Washington's first inauguration on April 30, 1789, which took place on the balcony of Federal Hall in New York City.*

OLD CITY HALL WALL ST. N.Y. 1789.

ABOVE: *A lithograph by George Holland showing a view down Wall Street of Federal Hall in New York City as it appeared in 1797. The first Congress met here from 1789 to 1790.*

there be added amendments that spelled out the rights guaranteed to the citizens. These two states were by no means alone in their concern; from the outset of the Constitutional Convention, many delegates speaking both on their own behalf or for the sense of their state's citizenry, were calling for written guarantees of various personal freedoms. And some states only voted to ratify the Constitution when they were assured that there would be such amendments. It was James Madison, himself a supporter of a strong federal government, who took the lead in drafting the amendments, and it was one of the first acts of Congress to submit the amendments to the states on September 25, 1789. It would be December 15, 1791, before enough states had ratified the first ten that would thereafter become known as the Bill of Rights.

Another early task before Congress was to establish the various departments that would become the executive branch, and this they did starting in July 1789. It was then left to President Washington to appoint the heads of these departments, which he began to do in September. The men Washington picked were all men he personally knew and trusted: Thomas Jefferson was named secretary of state; Alexander Hamilton, secretary of the treasury; Henry Knox, secretary of war; and Edmund Randolph, attorney general. Congress also established a federal court system, with a six-man Supreme Court, and Washington selected John Jay as its chief justice.

It would be 1793 before James Madison first referred to the group of department heads as "the cabinet," and in fact Washington did not call them together for meetings until near the end of his first term. Rather he relied on written opinions, and allowed each man to go pretty much his own way. But if there was one man who could be called "first among equals," it was Alexander Hamilton. His close relationship with Washington went back to the early days of the Revolutionary War and had continued ever since, even though they were quite different in many ways. Washington was an Olympian figure—older, restrained, dignified, and remote from the infighting that soon embroiled the leaders of the nation. And if Washington was Zeus, Hamilton was Hermes—young, dynamic, ambitious, and quick to enter the partisan fray.

Hamilton, a staunch believer in a strong central government, would dash off proposal after proposal for the federal government's taking the lead in such matters as assuming the states' debts from the Revolutionary War, imposing import duties and excise taxes, and supporting manufacturing. Behind and supporting their legal and technical details, moreover, were often broad and far-reaching principles. Perhaps the most notable of these was in Hamilton's 1791 proposal to establish a national bank, "Opinion on

The Bill of Rights
Adopted 1791

ARTICLE I After the first enumeration required by the first article of the Constitution, there shall be one representative for every thirty thousand, until the number shall amount to one hundred, after which the proportion shall be so regulated by Congress, that there shall be not less than one hundred representatives, nor less than one representative for every forty thousand persons, until the number of representatives shall amount to two hundred; after which the proportion shall be so regulated by Congress, that there shall be not less than two hundred representatives, nor more than one representative for every fifty thousand persons.

ARTICLE II No law varying the compensation for the services of the Senators and Representatives, shall take effect, until an election of Representatives shall have intervened.

ARTICLE III Congress shall make no law respecting an establishment of religion, or prohibiting the free exercise thereof; or abridging the freedom of speech, or of the press; or the right of the people peaceably to assemble, and to petition the Government for a redress of grievances.

ARTICLE IV A well regulated Militia, being necessary to the security of a free State, the right of the people to keep and bear Arms, shall not be infringed.

ARTICLE V No Soldier shall, in time of peace be quartered in any house, without the consent of the Owner, nor in time of war, but in a manner to be prescribed by law.

ARTICLE VI The right of the people to be secure in their persons, houses, papers, and effects, against unreasonable searches and seizures, shall not be violated, and no Warrants shall issue, but upon probable cause, supported by Oath or affirmation, and particularly describing the place to be searched, and the persons or things to be seized.

ARTICLE VII No person shall be held to answer for a capital, or otherwise infamous crime, unless on a presentment or indictment of a Grand Jury, except in cases arising in the land or naval forces, or in the Militia, when in actual service in time of War or public danger; nor shall any person be subject for the same offence to be twice put in jeopardy of life or limb; nor shall be compelled in any criminal case to be a witness against himself, nor be deprived of life, liberty, or property, without due process of law; nor shall private property be taken for public use, without just compensation.

ARTICLE VIII In all criminal prosecutions, the accused shall enjoy the right to a speedy and public trial, by an impartial jury of the State and district wherein the crime shall have been committed, which district shall have been previously ascertained by law, and to be informed of the nature and cause of the accusation; to be confronted with the witnesses against him; to have compulsory process for obtaining witnesses in his favor, and to have the Assistance of Counsel for his defence.

ARTICLE IX In Suits at common law, where the value in controversy shall exceed twenty dollars, the right of trial by jury shall be preserved, and no fact tried by a jury, shall be otherwise re-examined in any Court of the United States, than according to the rules of the common law.

ARTICLE X Excessive bail shall not be required, nor excessive fines imposed, nor cruel and unusual punishments inflicted.

ARTICLE XI The enumeration in the Constitution, of certain rights, shall not be construed to deny or disparage others retained by the people.

ARTICLE XII The powers not delegated to the United States by the Constitution, nor prohibited by it to the States, are reserved to the States respectively, or to the people.

the Constitutionality of the Bank of the United States." Tucked into its long and dense argument for such a specialized institution was Hamilton's assertion that the Constitution allowed the federal government "implied powers." That is, that just because many specifics were not mentioned or anticipated by the Constitution, it did not mean that Congress could not make laws relating to these matters.

The concept of "implied powers" was only one of many notions, proposals, words, and actions of Hamilton that antagonized those who did not believe in such a strong federal government. Hamilton and those who held much the same position were known as Federalists, while those who opposed him became known as Republicans. And although the dividing line was not absolute, the Federalists tended to come from the northern states with larger urban centers and with more industry and commerce, while the Republicans tended to be from the southern states, with smaller cities and more reliance on agriculture and more dependence on slaves (although this issue was temporarily set aside in the increasingly more bitter disputes between these two groups, the Federalists and Republicans). And it did not help matters that the leader of the Republicans was Thomas Jefferson, a member of Washington's cabinet as well as one of Washington's Virginian friends. Washington's first administration had barely begun when Jefferson and Hamilton began to engage in open warfare, each using their friends and supporters in and out of government to try to undermine the other, each sponsoring a newspaper that attacked the other. Washington did his best to try to paper over these differences but even he could not stop this slowly widening partisanship.

Among the many developments that aggravated this spilt was the Jay Treaty. There were still many disputes between the United States and Britain left unresolved by the Peace Treaty of 1783, when in 1793 Britain and France began to engage in open warfare. Britain then declared it had

Behold a Fabric now to Freedom rear'd,
Approv'd by Friends, and ev'n by Foes rever'd;
Where Justice, too, and Peace, by us ador'd,
Shall heal each Wrong, and keep ensheath'd the Sword
Approach then, Concord, fair Columbia's Son,
And, faithful Clio, write that WE ARE ONE.

the right to seize American merchant vessels carrying supplies to France. Despite this, Hamilton believed that the United States should not be taking sides against Britain; Jefferson believed just as strongly that the United States should side with France. Hamilton was closer to Washington and persuaded him to adopt a policy of neutrality, even to send John Jay, chief justice of the Supreme Court to England to negotiate a treaty with Britain that would clear up many of the outstanding disputes while putting a stop to the seizures. Jay did just this, signing the treaty on November 19, 1794. Jefferson resigned as secretary of state that December, but when the treaty was published in the United States early in 1795, the Jeffersonian Republicans were outraged—even taking to the streets, stoning Hamilton, and attacking the British embassy.

Hamilton himself resigned as secretary of the treasury in January 1795 for personal reasons, but continued to remain as an informal adviser to Washington. The Federalist-Republican disputes continued to rage and the Republicans even openly attacked Washington. So it was, as he moved into his final months in office, that he decided to release for publication in a Philadelphia newspaper on September a "farewell address" that he had actually first drawn up when he intended to retire after one term. Although both Hamilton and Jay made some suggestions, the address clearly expressed Washington's very strong personal sentiments. One was his refusal to stay on in a third term, this setting the tradition that would survive until Franklin Delano Roosevelt and the subsequent adoption of the Twenty-Second Amendment (1951). Another was his warning against foreign "alliances." But above all, he lamented the emergence of political parties. Founding Father, Washington undeniably was, but even he could not dictate the future course of the nation.

RIGHT: *The Jay Treaty of 1794 between the United States and England was so unpopular that enraged Jeffersonians hanged and burned its negotiator, John Jay, in effigy.*

George Washington

1732–1799

OPPOSITE: *A portrait of George Washington by artist Gilbert Stuart. Washington sat for Stuart a total of three times between 1795 and 1796.*

BELOW: *George Washington on horseback, by artist Henry Alexander Ogden. The portrait includes the flags of the states, and arms and currency of the period.*

FLAGS, UNIFORMS, CURRENCY AND ARMS OF THE REVOLUTION

Americans call George Washington "Father of his Country," and he richly deserves the title. Without stretching the metaphor, it is possible to say that he planted the seed, watered the sapling, and nurtured the growing tree to self-sufficiency.

The son of a Virginia planter, Washington became a surveyor at age seventeen, a land speculator at eighteen, and a militia major at twenty. Leading forty colonial soldiers and a few Indians into the Ohio River valley on a May 28, 1754, "peace" mission, he destroyed a French and Indian contingent and built a reputation. "I heard the bullets whistle, and believe me, there is something charming in the sound," he wrote a younger brother in a dispatch published throughout the colonies and reaching London.

But shortly afterward, Washington was forced to surrender Pennsylvania's Fort Necessity to a larger French force after a withering barrage killed one-third of his men and a flood washed out the fortification. Allowed to take his troops home, Washington returned to Virginia with his reputation intact. Volunteering for the French and Indian War the following year, Washington was appalled when General Edward Braddock of Britain insisted in a frontal attack after Washington warned him that the enemy would use guerilla tactics. Braddock and most of his British officers were killed near Fort Duquesne, Pennsylvania, while Washington and other survivors escaped. By the war's end in 1763, Washington had gained valuable fighting experience and resented the widespread discrimination against American officers.

Between wars, Washington married widow Martha Dandridge Custis and built his estate's value to more than 23,000 pounds (about $1.5 million in 2005 dollars) by diversifying beyond tobacco to wheat, lumber, and bricks, and teaching crafts to his skilled slaves. Remaining a public figure, he served as assemblyman, county justice and vestryman, and entertained some 2,000 guests over a six-year period. Washington attended the 1774 Continental Congress as a militant colonial, and as the best-known soldier in America he was the logical candidate to command the troops.

By the time Washington took command of the rebel troops on the Cambridge, Massachusetts, common in 1775, he was every inch the perfect American general. He had extensive military experience, he had come to hate the British, and at a broad-shouldered six feet three inches tall, he towered over almost all his troops. He assumed command in a buff and blue uniform, and his task looked every bit as imposing. The continental troops were poorly trained and constantly turning over, because their enlistments expired after a few months. But for the next six years, Washington kept the army intact with stiff discipline, occasional corporal punishment and his own shining example astride a white horse. "I thought...that I had never beheld so superb a man," the Marquis de Lafayette, his French aide-de-camp, recalled later.

Against the overwhelming superiority of the British army and navy—not to mention 17,000 Hessian mercenaries the enemy imported—Washington had poor prospects in head-to-head combat. What he did have was a strategy: keeping his troops together until the British wore down. "[W]e should on all Occasions avoid a general Action, or put anything to the Risque, unless compelled by necessity, into which we ought never be drawn," he wrote.

BELOW: *A painting depicting George Washington taking command of the Revolutionary Army under an elm tree in Cambridge, Massachusetts, on July 3, 1775. The event would become the inspiration for the poem,* Under the Washington Elm, *by Oliver Wendell Holmes. The elm tree stood for another 150 years.*

ABOVE: A portrait of General George Washington and the Marquis de Lafayette on horseback during the harsh winter of 1777–1778 in Valley Forge, Pennsylvania, by artist John Ward Dunsmore.

In January of 1776, Washington drove the British out of Boston Harbor by mounting cannon and mortar on Dorchester Heights. When the war shifted south, he was badly beaten in Brooklyn Heights, but escaped with most of his troops. The battle set a trend: lose on the field but survive to fight again.

Driven out of New York to a bitterly cold winter on the Pennsylvania side of the Delaware River, Washington led a force of 2,400 men across the river on December 26, 1776, routed a Hessian force in Trenton, New Jersey, and beat a pursuing British army at Princeton. After Benedict Arnold and Horatio Gates's forces stopped the British in Saratoga, New York, the next year, France allied itself with America. Nonetheless, Washington spent a cold winter in Valley Forge, Pennsylvania, and had to thwart Gates's attempt to dislodge him as commander in chief. Congress granted Washington extraordinary powers, but he enhanced his reputation by refusing to use them. He understood that without popular support and a lawful cause, he couldn't keep the union together. Congress went bankrupt, Arnold turned traitor, the underpaid and often starving troops twice mutinied, but Washington persisted through several more difficult years.

In 1781, he faked an attack on New York City, pinning many British troops there, then joined his French allies to force the final British surrender in Yorktown, Virginia. When Washington resigned rather than usurp power over the country that worshiped him, his reputation spread throughout the western world. Thomas Jefferson commented: "The moderation and virtue of one man probably prevented the Revolution from being closed by a subversion of the liberty it was intended to establish."

For the first of many times, Washington was called "Father of his Country." Again he returned to Virginia. Again the nation recalled him. The Treaty of Paris was signed in 1783, but Americans remained restless. Troops returned home, only to find their wartime scrip worthless and themselves overwhelmed by property and poll taxes. Writing about Shays's Rebellion in Massachusetts, Superintendent of War Henry Knox hyperbolically told Washington that 12,000 to 15,000 rebels intended to redistribute all property. Washington was sufficiently alarmed that he agreed to preside over the 1787 Constitutional Convention in Philadelphia.

Washington took little action at the convention, but his presence assured it of respectability and his signature on the Constitution—with an aside that it would need amendments—helped supporters win its ratification. In gratitude and effectively unanimously, the citizens of the new nation elected Washington first president of the United States.

There were still roiling currents beneath the ship of state—divisions between the northern and southern states, animosity between the emerging Federalist and Republican parties—but Washington's leadership kept it on course. His wise choices for leadership positions—John Jay at the Supreme Court, Jefferson at State, Alexander

ABOVE: *A French portrait of George Washington, engraved by Noël Le Mire. Washington holds copies of the Declaration of Independence and the Treaty of Alliance with France, while at his feet lie torn documents of reconciliation with Great Britain.*

FRAUNCES' TAVERN.

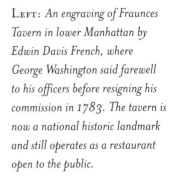

LEFT: *An engraving of Fraunces Tavern in lower Manhattan by Edwin Davis French, where George Washington said farewell to his officers before resigning his commission in 1783. The tavern is now a national historic landmark and still operates as a restaurant open to the public.*

Farewell Address
September 17, 1796

FRIENDS AND FELLOW-CITIZENS:

The period for a new election of a citizen, to administer the executive government of the United States, being not far distant, and the time actually arrived, when your thoughts must be employed designating the person, who is to be clothed with that important trust, it appears to me proper, especially as it may conduce to a more distinct expression of the public voice, that I should now apprize you of the resolution I have formed, to decline being considered among the number of those out of whom a choice is to be made....

In contemplating the causes, which may disturb our Union, it occurs as matter of serious concern, that any ground should have been furnished for characterizing parties by Geographical discriminations, Northern and Southern, Atlantic and Western; whence designing men may endeavour to excite a belief, that there is a real difference of local interests and views. One of the expedients of party to acquire influence, within particular districts, is to misrepresent the opinions and aims of other districts.....

To the efficacy and permanency of your Union, a Government for the whole is indispensable. No alliances, however strict, between the parts can be an adequate substitute; they must inevitably experience the infractions and interruptions, which all alliances in all times have experienced....

All obstructions to the execution of the Laws, all combinations and associations, under whatever plausible character, with the real design to direct, control, counteract, or awe the regular deliberation and action of the constituted authorities, are destructive of this fundamental principle, and of fatal tendency. They serve to organize faction, to give it an artificial and extraordinary force; to put, in the place of the delegated will of the nation, the will of a party, often a small but artful and enterprising minority of the community; and, according to the alternate triumphs of different parties, to make the public administration the mirror of the ill-concerted and incongruous projects of faction, rather than the organ of consistent and wholesome plans digested by common counsels, and modified by mutual interests....

There is an opinion, that parties in free countries are useful checks upon the administration of the Government, and serve to keep alive the spirit of Liberty. This within certain limits is probably true; and in Governments of a Monarchical cast, Patriotism may look with indulgence, if not with favor, upon the spirit of party. But in those of the popular character, in Governments purely elective, it is a spirit not to be encouraged.....

The great rule of conduct for us, in regard to foreign nations, is, in extending our commercial relations, to have with them as little political connexion as possible. So far as we have already formed engagements, let them be fulfilled with perfect good faith. Here let us stop.....

It is our true policy to steer clear of permanent alliances with any portion of the foreign world; so far, I mean, as we are now at liberty to do it; for let me not be understood as capable of patronizing infidelity to existing engagements. I hold the maxim no less applicable to public than to private affairs, that honesty is always the best policy. I repeat it, therefore, let those engagements be observed in their genuine sense. But, in my opinion, it is unnecessary and would be unwise to extend them....

LEFT: *An allegory mourning the death of George Washington on December 14, 1799. The poem reads, "Colombia lamenting the loss of her son/Who redeem'd her from slavery & liberty won/While Fame is directed by Justice to spread/The sad tidings afar that Washington's dead."*

Hamilton at Treasury, Henry Knox at War, Edmund Randolph at Justice, and Samuel Osgood at the U.S. Post Office among more than 1,000 offices—occupied Washington during his first term (1789–1793).

Although he intended to retire, Washington remained president for a second term to forestall domestic disharmony and deal with the revolutionary wars in France and with growing disputes with Britain over western territories. Washington remained neutral, which led to pro-France "Democratic-Republican societies" that opposed him and eventually created a formal opposition party to Washington's Federalist party. In Pennsylvania, Washington put down the so-called Whiskey Rebellion over liquor taxes without a single shot being fired, then typically pardoned all the protesters. His troops under General "Mad Anthony" Wayne defeated an Indian force at the Battle of Fallen Timbers. Washington barely got a bitterly divided Congress to approve the 1794 Jay Treaty that removed Great Britain from northwestern posts, but failed to prevent its impressment of American sailors. Late in the second term, Washington sent Thomas Pinckney to Madrid to negotiate an outlet to the sea via the Mississippi River.

Historians have described President Washington as more like a monarch than a chief executive. Riding in a horse-drawn coach, receiving callers at the White House as for a royal reception, he was widely deferred to and he achieved every one of his major goals except a national university and a Potomac canal. Washington's remote and autocratic style of leadership would be unacceptable today, but his prestige maintained a fragile national unity. When he retired for good in 1796, he issued a farewell address warning citizens against the "baleful effects" of party strife and asking them to "cherish public credit" but use it "as sparingly as possible." His speech, originally written in 1792, was widely viewed as isolationist, but in reality it asked for abstention from international conflicts for the next two decades. Not counting an undeclared war with France in the late 1790s and sparring with the Barbary pirates in the early 1800s, he essentially got his wish, because his successors kept the peace until the War of 1812.

Alone among the slaveholding Founding Fathers from Virginia, Washington freed his slaves—albeit, not effective until the death of his wife. Washington died at his home in Mount Vernon only days before the dawning of the nineteenth century, survived by his widow and no children. But he had fathered a grateful nation. Wrote Jefferson: "His was the singular destiny and merit of leading the armies of his country successfully through an arduous war for the establishment of its independence, of conducting its councils through the birth of a government, new in its forms and principles, until it settled down into a quiet and orderly train; and of scrupulously obeying the laws through the whole of his career, civil and military, of which the history of the world furnishes no other example."

BELOW: *A Childs and Inman lithograph of Mount Vernon, George Washington's estate in Virginia, which covered some eight thousand acres, divided into five separate farms. Washington is entombed in the family vault at the estate.*

Alexander Hamilton

1755/57–1804

Alexander Hamilton, honored as one of the most brilliant of Founding Fathers, was feared and reviled by many in his time. His brilliance was apparent from the first. Documents suggest that Hamilton was born on the island of Nevis in 1755, but Hamilton himself cited 1757 as his birth year. If so, then Hamilton was nine years old when he joined a merchant house as a clerk, and fourteen when he was placed in charge during the absence of his employer, Nicholas Cruger, for four months.

Hamilton's origins were inauspicious. He and his brother had been born out of wedlock to Rachel Faucett. James Hamilton, a Scottish bankrupt, abandoned the family in 1765, and Rachel died in 1768. Hamilton's preciosity, however, caused Cruger and Reverend Hugh Knox to arrange for his education in America. In 1773, he attended King's College, now Columbia University, in New York City, and graduated within a year.

In 1774, while still in college, Hamilton anonymously wrote *A Full Vindication of the Measures of Congress,* an essay so brilliant that many assumed it to be the work of John Jay. During the pre-revolutionary period, Hamilton addressed impromptu public gatherings, events that threatened to degenerate into violence. He counseled reason and civility, but when a printer's office

OPPOSITE: A portrait of Alexander Hamilton by artist John Trumbull. Hamilton's brilliance was such that an essay he wrote as a teenager at King's College was mistakenly attributed to John Jay, then a delegate to the Continental Congress.

BELOW: A stereograph of the birthplace of Alexander Hamilton on the island of Nevis, in the British West Indies. Hamilton was sent to study in America in 1773.

20514—Birthplace of Hamilton, Island of Nervis, B.W.I.

On the Constitutionality of the Bank of the United States
1791

The Secretary of the Treasury having perused with attention the papers containing the opinions of the Secretary of State and Attorney General, concerning the constitutionality of the bill for establishing a National Bank, proceeds, according to the order of the President, to submit the reasons which have induced him to entertain a different opinion.....

The first of these arguments is, that the foundation of the Constitution is laid on this ground: "That all powers not delegated to the United States by the Constitution, nor prohibited to it by the States, are reserved for the States, or to the people." Whence it is meant to be inferred, that Congress can in no case exercise any power not Included in those not enumerated in the Constitution....

It is not denied that there are implied as well as express powers, and that the former are as effectually delegated as the latter. And for the sake of accuracy it shall be mentioned, that there is another class of powers, which may be properly denominated resting powers. It will not be doubted, that if the United States should make a conquest of any of the territories of its neighbors, they would possess sovereign jurisdiction over the conquered territory. This would be rather a result, from the whole mass of the powers of the government, and from the nature of political society, than a consequence of either of the powers specially enumerated.....

The expediency of exercising a particular power, at a particular time, must, indeed depend on circumstances, but the constitutional right of exercising it must be uniform and invariable, the same to-day as to-morrow. It is essential to the being of the national government, that so erroneous a conception of the meaning of the word necessary should be exploded. It is certain that neither the grammatical nor popular sense of the term requires that construction. According to both, necessary often means no more than needful, requisite, incidental, useful, or conducive to. It is a common mode of expression to say, that it is necessary for a government or a person to do this or that thing, when nothing more is intended or understood, than that the interests of the government or person require, or will be promoted by, the doing of this or that thing. The imagination can be at no loss for exemplifications of the use of the word in this sense. And it is the true one in which it is to be understood as used in the Constitution. The whole turn of the clause containing it indicates, that it was the intent of the Convention, by that clause, to give a liberal latitude to the exercise of the specified powers. The expressions have peculiar comprehensiveness. They are thought to make all laws necessary and proper for carrying into execution the foregoing powers, and all other powers vested by the Constitution in the government of the United States, or in any department or officer thereof....

The truth is, that difficulties on this point are inherent in the nature of the Federal Constitution; they result inevitably from a division of the legislative power. The consequence of this division is, that there will be cases clearly within the power of the national government; others, clearly without its powers; and a third class, which will leave room for controversy and difference of opinion, and concerning which a reasonable latitude of judgment must be allowed....

ABOVE: *Captain Alexander Hamilton's artillery unit prepares for the Battle of Trenton on December 25, 1776. Also present at the battle, fighting alongside George Washington, was a future president, James Monroe, who was wounded.*

was ransacked at Hanover Square, his aversion to mob rule became fixed. In 1775 he wrote *The Farmer Refuted*, in which he identified the foundation of the new nation to be its almost limitless economic potential. Within two years of his arrival from the West Indies, Hamilton had sounded the enduring themes that would guide him in the founding of a nation.

At the outbreak of hostilities in 1775, Hamilton joined an artillery unit, to which he was appointed captain. In 1777, he became a lieutenant colonel on General Washington's staff. Over the next four years, Hamilton made a positive impression on Washington, although in 1781 the two quarreled, and Hamilton impulsively resigned. Washington and Hamilton reconciled, and Hamilton saw action at Yorktown. During his service, Hamilton observed Washington's struggle to wage war under constraints imposed by Congress; moreover, the wartime debts that threatened the states reinforced Hamilton's attention to the economic foundations of nationhood.

In 1780, Hamilton enhanced his status when he married Elizabeth Schuyler, daughter of the powerful New York landholder Philip Schuyler. Hamilton studied law, collected taxes, and was elected to the Confederation Congress from 1782 to 1783, during which time the Revolution came to an end. As the nation struggled, Hamilton saw the deficiencies of confederation. He returned to law, in one case defending the property rights of former

loyalists, a position that won him few friends. Hamilton moved in the highest circles of New York finance, and in 1784 he helped found the Bank of New York.

The Annapolis Convention of 1786 sought to address the nation's deteriorating situation. Hamilton was a member of the New York delegation, one of five states to attend, and he helped draft a statement that identified the social and economic problems that had permitted Daniel Shays's Rebellion and other regional insurrections to occur. Hamilton called for a Constitutional Convention of all the states.

In 1787, the Constitutional Convention convened in Philadelphia and Hamilton attended. The other members of the New York delegation, John Lansing and Robert Yates, were allies of New York's governor, George Clinton. Clinton opposed the strong national government that Hamilton envisioned, since its power would come at his expense. Hamilton was outvoted by Clinton's allies, and even when the gentlemen quit the convention, Hamilton chose not to cast his vote on behalf of the state of New York.

Hamilton strongly opposed the Virginia Plan, which favored direct election of a bicameral congress, thus privileging larger states; with even greater force, he opposed the New Jersey Plan, which sought to preserve state power. It wasn't until June 18, 1787, that he finally rose to present his plan. Those assembled, patriots all, were as steeped in principles of British

ABOVE: Leaders of the Continental Congress, by artist Augustus Tholey. From left to right: John Adams, Gouverneur Morris, Alexander Hamilton, and Thomas Jefferson.

governance as Hamilton, but no one supported his call for a Senate based on the House of Lords, whose members served for life. Hamilton also proposed that state governors and the national executive serve for life. In short, he called for the concentration of state power in the hands of an American aristocracy. As Hamilton had anticipated, his plan was dismissed. Once the Great Compromise, proposed by the Connecticut delegates had been achieved, Hamilton urged delegates to sign the Constitution as he did. For as Madison said of Hamilton, "No man's ideas were more remote from the plan than his own were thought to be."

Hamilton's greatest service to the Constitution came in the period of ratification. Hamilton, along with James Madison and John Jay, authored *The Federalist Papers*, a series of eighty-five essays, at least fifty-one of which Hamilton signed as "Publius." In his essays, he articulated the case for a strong federal government. Ratification was far from certain, since states such as New York would have to accommodate smaller, less powerful states. In 1788, Hamilton attended the Poughkeepsie Convention, where he led the fight for New York's ratification. When the debate began, Hamilton represented the minority position, but he persevered and won the day.

Hamilton's reached his zenith in 1789 when he became the nation's first secretary of the treasury under Washington. During the course of his term he would transform the government in fundamental ways and put the nation's fiscal house in order. He reported to Congress on the restoration of credit; the consolidation of debts; the formation of a national bank; and the necessity for developing manufacture. It was in his 1791 defense of establishing a national bank that Hamilton set forth his notion of "implied powers" in the Constitution, a concept that subsequent generations have continued to draw on for much of the legislation and many court rulings that support the development of the nation we know today.

RIGHT: *On the day that New York ratified the U.S. Constitution, July 26, 1788, Federalists celebrated with a parade featuring a float called the* Hamilton, *which was pulled by ten horses through the streets of lower Manhattan.*

Hamilton engaged in battles beyond the Treasury. In 1794, he donned his military uniform to join the federal troops in suppression of the Whiskey Rebellion. Hamilton also influenced foreign policy, counseling neutrality in European affairs and advising on treaties. His actions brought him into conflict with Thomas Jefferson, the secretary of state. Relations between the two grew so strained that Washington interceded to repair the breach.

Hamilton's rise was so rapid that Jefferson and Madison formed a second political party, the Republicans (today's Democrats), largely to oppose him in the event that he sought higher office. Ostensibly to provide for his family, Hamilton resigned from the Treasury post in 1795. Upon returning to the practice of law, Hamilton was a founder of the New York Manumission Society—a group advocating the freeing of slaves. He had been born to a slave-holding family, yet as early as 1779 Hamilton had suggested that slaves be recruited into the Revolutionary army in exchange for their freedom.

During his tenure at Treasury, Hamilton had engaged in an extra-marital affair with Maria Reynolds, who blackmailed him for years. To his reputation as a neo-monarchist, and the rumors that persisted regarding his parentage, the taint of sexual scandal was added. Hamilton acknowledged the last in *Observations on Certain Documents* (1797).

Hamilton founded the *New-York Evening Post*, today's *New York Post*. In that venue and others, he attacked John Adams, the nation's second president, a fellow Federalist. When Jefferson defeated Adams in the 1800 election, enraged Federalists sought to award the presidency to Aaron Burr, Jefferson's vice president, because Burr had received the same total of electoral votes. Jefferson, in Hamilton's opinion, was the lesser of two evils, and he threw his energy and prestige into defeating Burr. When Hamilton frustrated Burr's ambitions to become governor of New York in 1804, Burr challenged Hamilton to a duel. They met at Weehawken, New Jersey, where Hamilton's son, Philip, had been killed in a duel several years before. By most accounts, Hamilton fired in the air. Burr wounded Hamilton, mortally, and he died the next day.

A brilliant career had been terminated by a senseless death: Alexander Hamilton advocated his conservative principles, acted pragmatically to secure an effective government, and forged institutions that guided the American economy, and with it the nation, to unprecedented wealth and power.

John Jay

1745–1829

Opposite: A portrait of John Jay in judicial robes, engraved by Albert Rosenthal. Jay was appointed as the nation's first chief justice of the Supreme Court by President George Washington in 1789.

Above: An illustration from James Fenimore Cooper's novel, The Spy, featuring the fictional Harvey Birch and the real George Washington. Birch was said to be modeled on Enoch Crosby, a spy who worked counterintelligence operations with John Jay during the Revolution.

Descended from French Huguenots who had fled religious persecution, John Jay was born into a wealthy New York family in 1745. His upbringing reflected the values of his class, but privileged circumstances did not cause Jay to shrink from taking a major role in the birth and maturation of a new nation.

Jay graduated with highest honors from King's College (Columbia University) in 1764 and was admitted to the bar in 1768. He married Sarah Livingston, the daughter of William Livingston, later governor of New Jersey. In 1774, the Intolerable Acts, enacted by Britain in response to the Boston Tea Party, provoked Jay to join the New York Committee of Correspondence. He was opposed to immediate separation, but also distanced himself from the loyalists. Jay's actions were motivated by a desire to exercise a moderating influence upon more radical factions.

Even as he sought moderation, he composed the "Address to the People of Great Britain," in which he argued on behalf of the rights of the colonies. He attended both Continental Congresses and continued to urge reconciliation. Even after hostilities had started, he helped draft the Olive Branch Petition on July 8, 1775, but King George III rejected it out of hand. Jay chose to leave the Continental Congress in May 1776 to attend New York's provincial legislature from 1776 to 1777, so he was not present for the approval or signing of the Declaration of Independence. His ambivalence about independence is a matter of record.

During the month immediately before the signing of the Declaration, Jay led an investigation of a Tory plot to sabotage targets in New York City. The conspiracy implicated Royal Governor William Tyron and New York Mayor David Matthews; Jay also exposed a plot to kill or capture George Washington to pave the way for invasion. Acting in secrecy, Jay directed the

arrest of the plotters. The presence of 10,000 British troops in New York harbor in late June 1776 further concentrated Jay's mind, and he became a staunch supporter of Revolution. Well on into 1777, Jay continued to run a counterintelligence operation that used a number of spies; the most daring of these was Enoch Crosby, said to have been the model for Harvey Birch, hero of James Fenimore Cooper's novel, *The Spy*.

In 1777, Jay helped frame New York's state constitution. He was appointed the first chief justice of New York and served on the state's Council of Safety, a body empowered to act when the legislature was not in session. He was once again elected to the Continental Congress in 1778 and was voted president of that body, an office he held until 1779 when he sailed for Europe, where he would remain for four years. As minister to Spain, he sought recognition of his new nation and hoped to secure a loan. Spain provided neither, and Jay was embarrassed when Congress, assuming his success, spent hundreds of thousands of dollars it did not have.

In the spring of 1782, Jay joined Benjamin Franklin and John Adams in negotiating the Treaty of Paris. The rivalry between the European powers slowed negotiations, so Jay and his colleagues resorted to separate consultations with the British, a decision that caused controversy at home. A preliminary agreement was achieved in November 1782, in which the British acknowledged

ABOVE: *An unfinished painting by Benjamin West meant to commemorate the Treaty of Paris. From left to right: John Jay, John Adams, Benjamin Franklin, Henry Laurens, and William Temple Franklin. British commissioners, however, refused to sit for the painting.*

Treaty of Amity, Commerce, and Navigation
Concluded: November 19, 1794
Proclaimed: February 29, 1796

Articles:

His Britannic Majesty and the United States of America, being desirous, by a treaty of amity, commerce and navigation, to terminate their difference in such a manner, as, without reference to the merits of their respective complaints and pretentions, may be the best calculated to produce mutual satisfaction and good understanding; and also to regulate the commerce and navigation between their respective countries, territories and people, in such a manner as to render the same reciprocally beneficial and satisfactory; they have, respectively, named their Plenipotentiaries, and given them full powers to treat of, and conclude the said treaty,...Who have agreed on and concluded the following articles:

ARTICLE I.

There shall be a firm, inviolable and universal peace, and a true and sincere friendship between His Britannic Majesty, his heirs and successors, and the United States of America; and between their respective countries, territories, cities, towns and people of every degree, without exception of persons or places....

Lastly. This treaty, when the same shall have been ratified by His Majesty and by the President of the United States, by and with the advice and consent of their Senate, and the respective ratifications mutually exchanged, shall be binding and obligatory on His Majesty and on the said States, and shall be by them respectively executed and observed with punctuality and the most sincere regard to good faith; and whereas it will be expedient, in order the better to facilitate intercourse and obviate difficulties, that other articles be proposed and added to this treaty, which articles, from want of time and other circumstances, cannot now be perfected, it is agreed that the said parties will, from time to time, readily treat of and concerning such articles, and will sincerely endeavor so to form them as that they may conduce to mutual convenience and tend to promote mutual satisfaction and friendship; and that the said articles, after having been duly ratified, shall be added to and make a part of this treaty. In faith whereof we, the undersigned Ministers Plenipotentiary of His Majesty the King of Great Britain and the United States of America, have signed this present treaty, and have caused to be affixed thereto the seal of our arms.

the United States as independent, ceded territory east of the Mississippi River (except for Florida), and granted important North Atlantic fishing rights—and in September 1783 the treaty was signed and sealed.

When he returned to Congress in 1784, Jay found that he had already been appointed secretary of foreign affairs, not the last time he would be given a position without his knowledge. In that role, he was faced with British and American violations of the Treaty of Paris, the resolution of which proved impossible. His frustration convinced him of the need for a federal government with greater power.

Although he did not attend the convention in Philadelphia where the Constitution was framed, Jay contributed to *The Federalist* in which he, Madison, and Hamilton argued for ratification. Jay wrote the second through the fifth essays, but took ill, and did not write another essay until number sixty-four. He also wrote "An Address to the People of New York," stating the Federalist case, and attended the state convention at which New York ratified the Constitution.

After Washington was inaugurated in 1789, Jay became the first chief justice to the Supreme Court. He established court rules, procedures, and protocol. He also established the principle of judicial impartiality when Hamilton requested that the Court rule against opponents of a bill that assumed state debts. The business of the court, Jay argued, was to rule on the constitutionality of cases, not lobby for a bill.

BELOW: *The Treaty of Paris was signed by both parties on November 30, 1782, but was not approved by Congress until April 15, 1783. Standing at left are John Jay and Benjamin Franklin.*

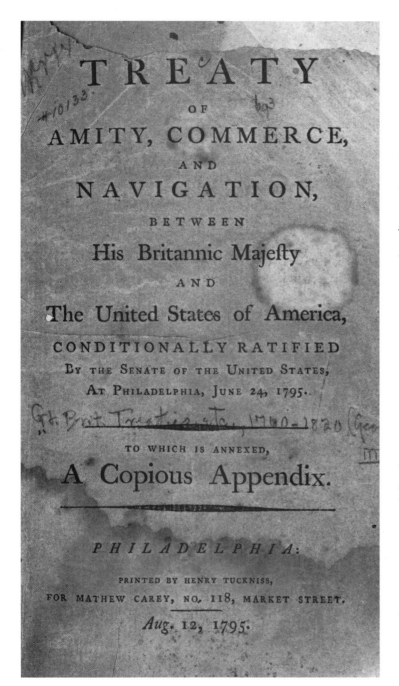

TREATY

OF

AMITY, COMMERCE,

AND

NAVIGATION,

BETWEEN

His Britannic Majesty

AND

The United States of America,

CONDITIONALLY RATIFIED

By the Senate of the United States,
At Philadelphia, June 24, 1795.

TO WHICH IS ANNEXED,

A Copious Appendix.

PHILADELPHIA:

PRINTED BY HENRY TUCKNISS,
FOR MATHEW CAREY, NO. 118, MARKET STREET.

Aug. 12, 1795.

ABOVE: *The Treaty of Amity (1794), also known as the Jay Treaty, earned its namesake much revulsion among his countrymen for what was seen as overly generous concessions made to the British.*

Three more cases marked Jay's tenure. In *Chisholm v. Georgia* the court ruled in favor of a citizen's right to sue a state or any other corporation. In *Georgia v. Brailsford*, the court established that the enforcement of treaties between the federal government and foreign powers fell outside state jurisdiction. The last, *Glass v. Sloop Betsy*, ruled that, without a treaty, representatives of foreign governments had no jurisdiction in the United States.

Jay took leave from the court when Washington assigned him to resolve a number of outstanding conflicts with Britain. For one, Britain had yet to pay reparations for slaves commandeered during the war; they also treated the Great Lakes region as their possession; as a final insult, the British boarded American ships and pressed American seamen into service. Jay resolved some conflicts, but not the practice of pressing Americans into the Royal Navy. The Jay Treaty, as it was called, satisfied few on this side of the Atlantic. So many effigies of him were burned that Jay claimed he could travel from Boston to Philadelphia by the light.

Once again Jay was elevated to an office he had not sought. During Jay's absence, Hamilton arranged his candidacy for governor of New York, an office to which Jay was elected before disembarking from the ship that had brought him home. In 1795, on account of this new responsibility, Jay retired from the Supreme Court, though he would have preferred to stay. As governor, Jay sought judicial reform, limited the death penalty, abolished flogging, and signed into law the gradual elimination of slavery. Jay did his best to eliminate corruption where he could, even when doing so upset his party.

John Jay retired from public life in 1801, but President John Adams tried to appoint him to a vacant seat on the Supreme Court. Jay declined. In his retirement, he became president of the American Bible Society, advocated for the anti-slavery movement, and kept abreast of agricultural reform. Jay lived until 1829, a long span during which he helped shepherd the nation from independence to governance.

PART FIVE

Handing Over a Nation

(1797–1801)

When John Adams assumed the presidency in 1797, it represented a personal triumph for a man who had taken a lead in founding the nation but who had since become so controversial and unpopular that it appeared he would never hold this office. And from the moment he did take office, the prospects for his administration were not promising. He had barely beaten Thomas Jefferson, his onetime colleague and friend, in the electoral college, and Jefferson, now his bitter political enemy, was vice president. Even Adams's own fellow Federalists were not that supportive of his views and goals. Meanwhile, the new nation found itself torn between its loyalty to France, the country that had effectively tipped the balance for the colonies in their revolutionary war, and its loyalty to England, still the nation with whom most Americans shared both families and values. The four years of the Adams presidency would not go easy. Indeed, they would prove to be years of tremendous turmoil, but by the same token, when his presidency ended and the nation remained intact, Adams could take some satisfaction in knowing that the foundation he had helped to lay was still solid.

Adams had not made things better by publishing—while vice president—a series of essays in the *Gazette of the United States* in 1790. These were eventually collected and published as *Discourses on Davila*. Henrico Davila was a once well-known Italian political philosopher and Adams used his writings as a structure on which to "hang" some of his own views on the nature of government. Unfortunately, some of his opinions could be interpreted as being virtually pro-monarchist and anti-populist, and the emergent Republicans who were gathering around Thomas Jefferson rushed to attack Adams. *The Gazette of the United States* was an unabashedly partisan supporter of the Federalists so Jefferson had backed the start of a new paper, the *National Gazette*, edited by

Philip Freneau: Rules for Changing a Limited Republican Government into an Unlimited Hereditary One
1782

1. It being necessary, in order to effect the change, to get rid of constitutional shackles and popular prejudices, all possible means and occasions are to be used for both these purposes.

2. Nothing being more likely to prepare the vulgar mind for aristocratical ranks and hereditary powers than titles, endeavor in the offset of the government to confer these on its most dignified officers. If the principle magistrate should happen to be particularly venerable in the eyes of the people, take advantage of that fortunate circumstance in setting the example....

5. As the novelty and bustle of inaugurating the government will for some time keep the public mind in a heedless and unsettled state, let the press during this period be busy in propogating the doctrines of monarchy and aristocracy....

10. "Divide and govern" is a maxim consecrated by the experience of ages, and should be as familiar in its use to every politician as the knife he carries in his pocket. In the work here to be executed, the best effects may be produced by this maxim, and with peculiar facility....

12. The expediency of seizing every occasion of external danger for augmenting and perpetuating the standing military force is too obvious to escape. So important is this matter that for any loss or disaster whatever attending the national arms, there will be ample consolation and compensation in the opportunity for enlarging the establishment. A military defeat will become a political victory, and the loss of a little vulgar blood contribute to ennoble that which flows in the veins of our future dukes and marquesses.

13. The same prudence will improve the opportunity afforded by an increase of military expenditures for perpetuating the taxes required for them....

15. As it is not to be expected that the change of a republic into a monarchy, with the rapidity desired, can be carried through without occasional suspicions and alarms, it will be necessary to be prepared for such events. The best general rule on the subject is to be taken from the example of crying "Stop thief" first—neither lungs nor pens must be spared in charging every man who whispers, or even thinks, that the revolution on foot is meditated, with being himself an enemy to the established government and meaning to overturn it. Let the charge be reiterated and reverberated till at last such confusion and uncertainty be produced that the people, being not able to find out where the truth lies, withdraw their attention from the contest.

Many other rules of great wisdom and efficacy might be added; but it is conceived that the above will be abundantly enough for the purpose. This will certainly be the case if the people can be either kept asleep so as not to discover, or be thrown into artificial divisions so as not to resist, what is silently going forward....

a staunch Republican and clever writer, Philip Freneau. Needless to say, Freneau was among those who attacked Adams, most notoriously in his satirical set of "rules" to convert the United States government into a monarchy.

If it had been only this kind of partisan wrangling over personal and abstract issues, that might have been one thing, but the growing split between the Federalists and Republicans was contaminating virtually all aspects of the Adams administration. In 1795, near the end of Washington's presidency, the Federalists had endorsed the treaty with Britain negotiated by John Jay. Although the treaty got Britain to agree to stop impressing, or seizing, sailors from American ships and to withdraw from their forts on the then northwestern frontier, many Americans felt that the treaty was far too favorable in other respects to the British.

This difference of opinion in turn was part of a larger disagreement among some Republicans and some Federalists—namely, whether the United States should show more support for France or for Britain, now at war. France was at this time in total disarray, with a revolution raging, and in any case, most Americans had little direct connections with a people who spoke a different language and had so many different ways. Great Britain, on the other hand, despite the recent war, spoke the same language and its institutions and customs, in fact, still underlay most Americans's lives. The Federalists, led by Alexander Hamilton, thus advocated stronger and friendlier relations with the British, while the Republicans, led by Jefferson, called for supporting France.

This disagreement had surfaced well before Adams took office. Washington, for instance, had sent James Monroe as ambassador to France in 1794, with the goal of at least maintaining friendly relations with the new revolutionary government of France. Monroe did his best, but in trying to maintain a neutral position, Washington only antagonized both the extreme Federalists and the extreme Republicans. Meanwhile, the French, angry at the United States for signing the Jay Treaty with Britain, now waged virtually

John Adams and Federalist-Controlled Congress
An Act for the Punishment of Certain Crimes Against the United States
July 14, 1798

SEC. 2. *And be it farther enacted,* **That if any person shall write, print, utter or publish, or shall cause or procure to be written, printed, uttered or published, or shall knowingly and willingly assist or aid in writing, printing, uttering or publishing any false, scandalous and malicious writing or writings against the government of the United States, or either house of the Congress of the United States, or the President of the United States, with intent to defame the said government, or either house of the said Congress, or the said President, or to bring them, or either of them, into contempt or disrepute; or to excite against them, or either or any of them, the hatred of the good people of the United States, or to stir up sedition within the United States, or to excite any unlawful combinations therein, for opposing or resisting any law of the United States, or any act of the President of the United States, done in pursuance of any such law, or of the powers in him vested by the constitution of the United States, or to resist, oppose, or defeat any such law or act, or to aid, encourage or abet any hostile designs of any foreign nation against United States, their people or government, then such person, being thereof convicted before any court of the United States having jurisdiction thereof, shall be punished by a fine not exceeding two thousand dollars, and by imprisonment not exceeding two years....**

ABOVE: *A 1789 American political cartoon regarding the XYZ affair, in which the five leaders of the French Revolution, known as the Directory, here represented as a five-headed man, threatens American commissioners at dagger's point.*

open war on American merchant ships, seizing cargoes and even impressing sailors. Hamilton called for war against France and Jefferson continued to speak out in favor of the French Revolution.

In this atmosphere and with his term barely six months old, Adams dispatched three America commissioners to Paris in September 1797 to negotiate a treaty to stop what would become known as the "quasi-war" with France. The French foreign minister, the famous Talleyrand, chose to allow three agents to negotiate with the Americans, and because the negotiations were supposed to be secret, the Americans and President Adams referred to them only as X., Y., and Z. It soon became apparent that these men expected essentially a bribe if there was to be any treaty. One of the Americans, Charles Pinckney, is said to have replied at one point, "It is No! No! Not a sixpence!" (Pinckney is often credited with having said, "Millions for defense, but not one cent for tribute." But this was actually said by Robert Goodloe Harper in a toast to John Marshall in June 1798.)

The American commissioners broke off negotiations in March 1798 and returned home, and when accounts of the so-called XYZ affair began to circulate in the United States, there was mounting outrage at the French. War now seemed imminent and Congress established a Department of the Navy and called for the construction of six "ships of the line," (among them the USS *Constitution*). Congress also persuaded George Washington to return to duty to command the army; he never did have to do anything but Hamilton—only too happy to make war against the French—got himself appointed Washington's chief assistant and took an active role. The war was conducted at sea between July 1798 and May 1800, but ended after Adams sent another delegation to Paris and this time they did negotiate a treaty with the new leader of France, Napoleon Bonaparte.

Adams could have emerged from this crisis fairly well, but in the meantime he gave more ammunition to his enemies by backing his fellow Federalists in Congress as they passed the infamous Alien and Sedition Acts of 1798 in response to continuing attacks by the Republicans on both Federalist policies and individuals. The Alien Acts authorized the president to imprison or even deport non-citizens with a simple order. The Sedition Act made it a crime to criticize the president, Congress, or the government. These acts caused a storm of protest throughout the country by any who saw them as violating the Bill of Rights, but inevitably it was the Republicans who mounted the strongest attacks. Jefferson himself drafted what became known as the Kentucky Resolutions, which went so far as to virtually call for a state to secede from the union in protest against such acts. James Madison wrote the Virginia Resolutions, which called the acts unconstitutional.

Although Adams never used the Alien Acts, he did allow for the arrest of several journalists who supported Jefferson. And although the acts would expire by 1801, the damage had been done. Intended to weakened Jefferson and his Republicans, instead they aroused strong feelings against Adams. In addition, some Federalists were angry at Adams for not declaring war against the French. As a result, in the election of 1800, John Adams lost and Thomas Jefferson ended up as president. But this did not stop Adams from one more act that would cement his image as a divisive president. In

ABOVE: *President John Adams commissioned Alexander Hamilton as inspector general of the army in 1798 at George Washington's behest. Though both Federalists, Hamilton was disappointed with Adams's leadership, a rift that helped lead to the election of Thomas Jefferson in 1800.*

LEFT: *After George Washington left office, Congress was often bitterly divided, as illustrated by a row between representatives Matthew Lyon, a Democrat–Republican from Vermont, and Roger Griswold, a Federalist from Connecticut, on the House floor, fought with cane and fireplace tongs. Not coincidentally, Lyon is the best known violator of the Sedition Act, actually serving four months in jail.*

Thomas Jefferson
The Kentucky Resolutions
Approved November 19, 1798

I. RESOLVED, That the several states composing the United States of America are not united on the principle of unlimited submission to their general government; but that, by compact, under the style and title of a Constitution for the United States, and of amendments thereto, they constituted a general government for special purposes, delegated to that government certain definite powers, reserving, each state to itself, the residuary mass of right to their own self-government; and that whensoever the general government assumes undelegated powers, its acts are unauthoritative, void, and of no force; that to this compact each state acceded as a state, and is an integral party; that this government, created by this compact, was not made the exclusive or final judge of the extent of the powers delegated to itself, since that would have made its discretion, and not the Constitution, the measure of its powers; but that, as in all other cases of compact among parties having no common judge, each party has an equal right to judge for itself, as well of infractions as of the mode and measure of redress....

3. RESOLVED, That it is true, as a general principle, and is also expressly declared by one of the amendments to the Constitution, that "the powers not delegated to the United States by the Constitution, nor prohibited by it to the states, are reserved to the states respectively, or to the people;" and that, no power over the freedom of religion, freedom of speech, or freedom of the press, being delegated to the United States by the Constitution, nor prohibited by it to the states, all lawful powers respecting the same did of right remain, and were reserved to the states, or to the people;.... That therefore the act of the Congress of the United States, passed on the 14th of July, 1798, entitled "An Act in Addition to the Act entitled 'An Act for the Punishment of certain Crimes against the United States,'" which does abridge the freedom of the press, is not law, but is altogether void, and of no force....

the weeks between the election and Jefferson's inauguration, he enlarged the federal court system and appointed John Marshall, a staunch Federalist, as the chief justice of the Supreme Court.

So it was that John Adams, despite the bitter feelings and language that disfigured his administration, turned over two of the main branches of the government to two men, Thomas Jefferson and John Marshall, who represented opposing views of the role of the federal government. Yet for all the controversies and passions and infighting that colored the four years of the Adams administration, something more important for the United States of America can be said to have emerged during those years. For one thing, they did not resort to violence against one another, they did not secede, they did not discard the Constitution nor disavow the Declaration of Independence. It might even be said that it was precisely because two such men as Thomas Jefferson and John Marshall could co-exist that the United States of America flourished. It turned out that the Founding Fathers had done their job well, by creating institutions that were both strong and flexible, and by providing the ideas that would inspire future generations.

John Adams

1735–1826

Among all the Founding Fathers, John Adams has been referred to as the "Father of Independence." The colonies surely would have separated from Great Britain without him, but not necessarily when and how they did.

A Harvard-educated lawyer, Adams was appointed town attorney in Braintree, Massachusetts, specifically to challenge the 1765 Stamp Act that taxed legal documents and publications. Adams and other spokesmen argued that the mother country couldn't tax people who weren't represented in Parliament, leading to the act's repeal in 1766. But the following year Adams again led the resistance—this time when Parliament passed the Townshend Acts of 1767, which taxed imports to the colonies.

Although Adams was a patriot, he was also an independent thinker. After the 1770 Boston Massacre, he defended eight British soldiers accused of murdering five citizens. Arguing that protesters ridiculed and threatened the soldiers into shooting, he said famously, "Facts are stubborn things." Adams won acquittals for six of the eight. His role did not please his fellow insurgents, but it convinced them he was a man of principle.

Adams supported later protests, including the 1773 Boston Tea Party, and spurned rapprochement with Great Britain after he was appointed to the first and second Continental Congresses. With the outbreak of fighting in 1775 during the second congress, Adams displayed his statesmanship by nominating a Virginian, George Washington, as commander in chief.

Adams's role in the Philadelphia deliberations of the Second Continental Congress during the summer of 1776 forever solidified his designation as a Founding Father. The men gathered there were by no means unified in breaking free of King George III and

The able Doctor, or America Swallowing the Bitter Draught.

Parliament. The delegates from New York, New Jersey, Pennsylvania, Delaware, South Carolina, and Maryland had been ordered earlier that year to vote against independence. A model of restraint "borne down" by his unpopularity, Adams nonetheless got delegates to agree unanimously in May that individual colonies should govern themselves. His use of what he called "rapid reason" wore down adversaries. As a British spy put it, Adams saw "large subjects largely."

On June 7, 1776, Richard Henry Lee of Virginia proposed a colony-wide declaration of independence, but Pennsylvania's John Dickinson and others objected. A Committee of Five—Thomas Jefferson, Benjamin Franklin, Roger Sherman, Robert Livingston, and Adams—was appointed to draft a tentative document.

On July 1, as rain pounded the windows outside the Pennsylvania State House (later renamed Independence Hall), a great debate began. The cautious Dickinson said breaking with Great Britain would be "to brave a storm in a skiff made of paper." Adams, who understood the horrors of Lexington and Concord, knew there was no turning back. His words weren't recorded, but they probably resembled those in a letter he wrote to a friend: "Objects of the most stupendous magnitude, measures in which the lives and liberties of millions, born and unborn are most essentially interested, are now before us. We are in the very midst of revolution, the most complete, unexpected, and remarkable of any in the history of the world." After nine hours—Adams speaking for two of these—Pennsylvania and South Carolina objected, New York abstained, and Delaware's two-man delegation was divided. The final vote was postponed a day.

On July 2, Caesar Rodney, a noted Delaware patriot, arrived in Philadelphia, making his delegation pro-independence. When Dickinson and ally Robert Morris absented themselves in deference to the prevailing mood, Pennsylvania voted 3-2 for secession. In the end, twelve states voted to break with Great Britain, and New York abstained. Technically, that consti-

Discourses on Davila
1790

AMIDST all their exultations, Americans and Frenchmen should remember that the perfectibility of man is only human and terrestrial perfectibility. Cold will still freeze, and fire will never cease to burn; disease and vice will continue to disorder, and death to terrify mankind. Emulation next to self-preservation will forever be the great spring of human actions, and the balance of a well-ordered government will alone be able to prevent that emulation from degenerating into dangerous ambition, irregular rivalries, destructive factions, wasting seditions, and bloody, civil wars....

The controversy between the rich and the poor, the laborious and the idle, the learned and the ignorant, distinctions as old as the creation, and as extensive as the globe, distinctions which no art or policy, no degree of virtue or philosophy can ever wholly destroy, will continue, and rivalries will spring out of them. These parties will be represented in the legislature, and must be balanced, or one will oppress the other. There will never probably be found any other mode of establishing such an equilibrium, than by constituting the representation of each an independent branch of the legislature, and an independent executive authority, such as that in our government, to be a third branch and a mediator or an arbitrator between them. Property must be secured, or

liberty cannot exist. But if unlimited or unbalanced power of disposing property, be put into the hands of those who have no property, France will find, as we have found, the lamb committed to the custody of the wolf. In such a case, all the pathetic exhortations and addresses of the national assembly to the people, to respect property, will be regarded no more than the warbles of the songsters of the forest. The great art of law-giving consists in balancing the poor against the rich in the legislature, and in constituting the legislative a perfect balance against the executive power, at the same time that no individual or party can become its rival.

The essence of a free government consists in an effectual control of rivalries. The executive and the legislative powers are natural rivals; and if each has not an effectual control over the other, the weaker will ever be the lamb in the paws of the wolf. The nation which will not adopt an equilibrium of power must adopt a despotism. There is no other alternative. Rivalries must be controlled, or they will throw all things into confusion; and there is nothing but despotism or a balance of power which can control them. Even in the simple monarchies, the nobility and the judicatures constitute a balance, though a very imperfect one, against the royalties....

tuted a unanimous vote. "[Adams's] power of thought and expression…moved us from our seats," Jefferson later declared.

That was not all Adams did. Historians differ on whether he appointed Jefferson to write the Declaration of Independence—Adams said yes, Jefferson claimed that he was unanimously chosen—but Adams clearly helped him edit it and defended him against pre-adoption attacks on its language. "No man better merited than Mr. John Adams to hold a most conspicuous place in the design," Jefferson wrote. "He was the pillar of its support on the floor of Congress, its ablest advocate and defender against the multifarious assaults encountered." The document was not signed until August 2, but Adams and Jefferson proclaimed July 4 Independence Day.

A View of the present Seat of his Excel. the Vice President of the United States.
The Society of Iconophiles
New York.
Re-engraved on copper
1901
by Sidney L. Smith.

By this time, Adams was looking abroad. During the Revolutionary War, he had gone to Paris to assist Benjamin Franklin in establishing an alliance, and he now persuaded the Netherlands to lend money to pay the national debt. The Netherlands and France were the only European powers to recognize the United States before the end of the War for Independence. In 1782, Adams returned to France, where he and Franklin began negotiating the 1783 Treaty of Paris that ended the Revolutionary War while giving Americans all territory to the Mississippi River.

After serving as the first ambassador to Great Britain and writing *A Defence of the Constitutions of Government of the United States of America* (1787), calling for a chief executive and strong central government for the public interest, Adams was elected George Washington's vice president in 1789. For the next eight years he did little more than cast a tie-breaking vote in the Senate and advocate Washington's policies. Adams called the vice presidency "the most insignificant office that ever the invention of man contrived or his imagination conceived."

While Washington governed almost as a king, getting virtually every concession he sought, politicians broke off into two bitterly feuding parties, the Federalists and the Republicans. Like Washington, Adams was a Federalist, and his former friend Jefferson led the Republicans. At the time, the candidate with the second most electoral votes became vice president. When Adams beat Jefferson 71-68 in the 1796 presidential election, America's first "Odd Couple," now overt enemies, took power.

ABOVE: *An engraving by Sidney L. Smith of the Richmond Hill House in Manhattan where John Adams lived as vice president. Adams called the vice presidency "the most insignificant office that ever the invention of man contrived."*

A stiff and prickly man better suited for thinking than governing, the short, stout, bald Adams had a difficult time as president. His four years were mired in disputes with former ally France. At war with Great Britain since 1795, France also began firing on U.S. ships in the Caribbean. In 1797, Adams sent three delegates to a peace parley in Paris but withdrew them after three French officials he called X., Y., and Z. demanded a $250,000 bribe. Following the XYZ affair, American politicians debated war with France. Adams's Federalists demanded it, while the minority Republicans fought it. In perhaps his greatest achievement as president, Adams continued negotiations until war was averted.

Unfortunately, the XYZ affair also produced Adams's worst moment in power. Yielding to his fellow Federalists, he signed the 1798 Alien and Sedition Acts, which allowed him to deport or imprison immigrants from nations considered hostile and virtually outlawed criticism in the press. The acts, widely ridiculed, were rarely enforced in their four years of life.

In 1800, Adams (undermined by fellow Federalist Alexander Hamilton) lost his bid for re-election to Jefferson. Determined to leave his mark, Adams appointed many Federalists to the bench and installed John Marshall as chief justice of the Supreme Court. Nonetheless, Adams left office so embittered that he did not bother attending his archenemy's inauguration.

He returned home to Quincy (formerly Braintree) and spent the rest of his life reading, studying and writing. Around 1812, he began a correspondence with Jefferson, and the two eventually reconciled. As they wrote about religion, aging, and politics, Adams declared, "You and I ought not to die, before we have explained ourselves to each other."

He rarely left his farm during his retirement, publicly emerging in 1820 when, in respect for his Jewish friends, the 85-year-old Adams urged the Massachusetts legislature to pass a freedom of religion amendment to its constitution. Although he received a standing ovation for attending, his request was denied.

When Adams died on July 4, 1826—the fiftieth anniversary of the adoption of the Declaration of Independence—his final words were supposedly, "Thomas Jefferson still survives." Though he did utter that thought on his last day of life, Adams outlived Jefferson by a few hours, and in his last recorded words gasped to his granddaughter Susanna, "Help me, child! Help me!" That was a reasonable request, since John Adams had already helped his country become the United States of America.

BELOW: *A 1799 decorative display by Amos Doolittle featuring President John Adams and the then sixteen United States. Joining the original thirteen states were Vermont (1791), Kentucky (1792), and Tennessee (1796).*

Timothy Pickering

1745–1829

During the Revolution, Timothy Pickering proved himself to be an expert of logistics, acting as the quartermaster general for the Continental army. But it was as secretary of war that Pickering emerged as not only an exceptional bureaucrat, but also a visionary, founding the young country's first military academy and overseeing the building of some of the nation's most famous warships.

Timothy Pickering was born in Salem, Massachusetts, in 1745. He graduated from Harvard and studied law before being admitted to the bar in 1768. Although he practiced law very little, Pickering did become involved in matters of local government, including selectman and town

RIGHT: *An etching of the silver medal presented to Sagoyewatha, also known as Red Jacket, a leader of the Seneca Indians, by President George Washington in 1792. Timothy Pickering helped negotiate treaties with various Native American tribes, including the Seneca.*

clerk, showing an ability for organization that would be the hallmark of his career. Pickering joined the Massachusetts militia, rising to the rank of colonel, where he exhibited a talent for military organization. In 1775, Pickering wrote a drill manual, *An Easy Plan of Discipline for a Militia.* The manual was widely used for instruction by the Continental army for many years.

Pickering's manual, along with his able service in the Massachusetts militia, brought him to the attention of General George Washington, who appointed now Colonel Pickering to the post of quartermaster general during the Revolution. The position was a showcase for Pickering's logistical abilities,

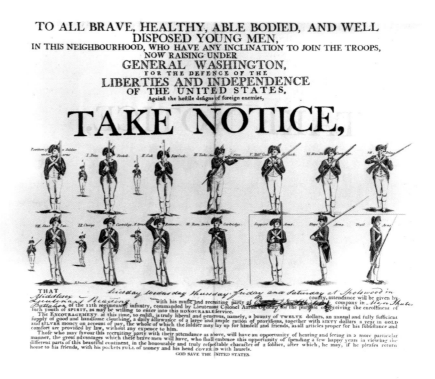

RIGHT: *A handbill soliciting recruits for the Continental army, circa 1775. Timothy Pickering's military training manual was one of the first of its kind in the colonies and was used to drill army recruits for many years.*

An Easy Plan of Discipline for a Militia
1775

Take care to perform the Manual Exercise! Every soldier must give the greatest attention to the words of command. He is to stand straight and firm upon his legs, with his heels close together, and toes a little turned out; the belly drawn in a little, but without constraint; the breast a little projected; the shoulders square to the front, and kept back; the head erect, and turned to the right, so as to look easily at the buglar; the right hand hanging straight down by the side with the palm towards the thigh, in its natural, unconstrained position; he is to carry the firelock against the left shoulder, almost upright, and so low down that the guard will be just under the left breast; the barrel outwards; the left elbow drawn back (but without constraint) and not thrust out from the side; the three last fingers of the left hand under the butt, and the forefinger and thumb on the fore side of it; thus grasping it strongly, and with the upper part of the palm of the hand pressing the piece to the side, that it may be kept steady; by this means bringing the backs of the fingers which are under the butt and turn up on the inside of it, close against the projecting top of the thigh-bone; and lastly turning the lock a very little to the front so that the piece may not lean towards the head nor from it.

I. Fix your Bayonet! 3 motions.
1. Keeping the firelock steady at the shoulder, seize it briskly with the right hand under the cock, the thumb on the side of the stock, and pointing upwards.
2. Throw up your left hand, and seize the firelock at the swell of the stock below the tail pipe, bringing your left arm, from the hand to the elbow, close along the outside of the firelock, which will be brought about four inches forwards from the shoulder, without moving the butt.

3. Quitting the right hand, with your left hand sink the firelock (letting it flip a little) on the left side till the butt strikes the ground, as far back as the heels; the muzzle coming about five inches before the hollow of the shoulder; the left arm is to be straight, the left hand holding the firelock a little above the swell of the tail pipe; at the same instant seizing the socket, or the handle of the bayonet with the right hand, (the curved neck of it coming between the thumb and fore finger) and the thumb in the hollow of the bend, draw it, and bringing the notch of the sight on the muzzle, thrust it down, turn it from you, (carrying your hand downwards) and fix it....

III. Charge your Bayonet! 2 motions.
1. Seize the firelock with the right hand below the cock, as in explanation 1st, motion 1st.
2. Make a half face to the right, turning upon both heels (keeping them both together) till the right toe points to the right, and the left toe to the front, at the same time giving the firelock a set-off by the butt, and quitting it with the left hand, bring it with the right hand to the right side, pulling up the butt briskly, thereby bringing the piece down with smartness upon the palm of the left hand, with which you meet it (just as it falls to a level) about half way between the hammer-spring and the tail-pipe, the thumb on the inside, pointing forwards, along the stock, the fingers clasped round the piece; with your right hand you grasp strongly the small of the stock behind the lock, pressing the piece to you, the back of the thumb touching the lowermost rib, the two last fingers bearing on the top of the hip; the bayonet is presented directly to the front, upon a level, the left hand supporting the firelock, to do it more easily, as well as strongly, press the left arm from the shoulder to the elbow, close to the body....

highlighted by Washington's unimpeded march from New York to Virginia for the siege of Yorktown, which proved to be the decisive battle of the Revolution. Washington's army was never detained during the march for want of supplies or transportation, but was continuously maintained in a feat of logistics credited to Pickering.

Following the Revolution, Pickering officially relocated to Pennsylvania, where he would later work to ratify the new federal Constitution. In 1789, President Washington appointed Pickering to formalize relations with the Seneca Indians. After years of work with the various tribes on the western frontiers, Pickering returned with the Canandaigua Treaty of 1794 signed by members of the Six Nations of Indians. Also at that time, Pickering served as the country's postmaster general.

In 1795, Washington appointed Pickering secretary of war. Pickering distinguished himself in that position by proposing the nation's first military academy, which was formally established at West Point in March 1802. Pickering was also in charge of the navy, where he oversaw the construction of a fleet of magnificent frigates, including the *Constitution*, the *United States*, and the *Constellation*. In 1795, Washington selected Pickering as his secretary of state, a position he continued to hold into the administration of John Adams. Pickering, however, was loyal to Alexander Hamilton, and was essentially fired by Adams in 1800 over disagreements with the administration.

Pickering returned to Massachusetts, where he was elected to the U.S. Senate and later the U.S. House of Representatives as a Federalist. Sometimes extreme in his views, Pickering was also a member of the Essex Junto, a group of radical Federalists that called for the secession of New England from the Union. Pickering died in Salem at the age of eighty-four. Although not widely remembered today, his steadfast service to the United States earned Pickering a rank among the nation's Founding Fathers.

RIGHT: *A view of the nation's first military academy, West Point (circa 1874), in upstate New York, which Timothy Pickering proposed during his term as President George Washington's secretary of war.*

Oliver Ellsworth

1745–1807

When the first Congress under the new Constitution convened on March 4, 1789, a key order of business was to pass legislation that defined the structure of the federal courts. The Constitution had clearly laid out the composition and responsibilities of the legislative and executive branches of government, but it had left vague the structure of the third branch, the judiciary. That task was left to a committee led by a man who had been instrumental in writing the Constitution itself, Oliver Ellsworth.

OPPOSITE: An engraving of Oliver Ellsworth after artist John Trumbull. Ellsworth is credited with writing the Judiciary Act of 1789, which laid out the framework for the nation's federal judicial system.

The son of a farmer, Oliver Ellsworth was born in Windsor, Connecticut, in 1745. With an aim to become a minister, Ellsworth studied theology, first at Yale and later at the College of New Jersey (later Princeton University), where he was swept up in the opposition to British taxation. With a strong desire to aid the forces of independence, Ellsworth switched his focus of study to law. He was admitted to the bar in 1771 and began a practice in Windsor, eventually moving to Hartford. He was elected to the Continental Congress in 1777 as a representative of Connecticut, serving for six annual terms. During the Revolution Ellsworth sat on a committee that financed the militia and was a member of the Council of Safety for Connecticut.

In 1787, Ellsworth was elected to the Constitutional Convention. His broad knowledge of jurisprudence was recognized by his fellow delegates and Ellsworth was elected a member of the committee charged with writing the first draft of the Constitution. Later when the convention deadlocked in a dispute between the large and small states over apportioning representation, it was Ellsworth, along with Roger Sherman, who proposed the Connecticut Compromise (also known as the Great Compromise). It called for a bicameral legislature, with one house based on a state's population and the other house with equal representation from all states. Despite his great contributions to the framing of the Constitution, Ellsworth was called away before negotiations were complete and did not sign the founding document. Nevertheless, Ellsworth did write a series of letters that were published in several Connecticut newspapers under the pseudonym "Landholder" in which he argued in favor of ratification.

Ellsworth was elected one of the first two U.S. Senators from Connecticut in 1789. He was selected to lead the committee that was charged with framing the structure of the federal courts, since Article III of the Constitution had been left vague on the subject. Ellsworth is credited as the main writer of the Judiciary Act of 1789, which laid out in detail the makeup and composition of the federal courts. Aside from a few minor alterations, the structure of the federal judiciary remains the same to this day.

Ellsworth also had a hand in "persuading" Rhode Island to ratify the Constitution. Rhode Island had been reluctant to join the Union, so a Senate bill was written that would require the state to immediately settle its share of the national debt if it did not ratify. Rhode Island begrudgingly joined the Union on May 29, 1790. Ellsworth later wrote to a friend, "The Constitution is now adopted by all the States and I have much satisfaction, and perhaps some vanity, in seeing, at length, a great work, finished, for which I have long labored incessantly."

In 1796, Ellsworth was appointed as the nation's second chief justice of the Supreme Court where he served for nearly five years. He then briefly acted as the commissioner to France before retiring back to Windsor in 1801. After a long career spent in dedication to his nation, Ellsworth enjoyed a quiet retirement writing occasional articles on farming until his death at the age of sixty-two.

LEFT: *An 1894 lithograph of the first eight chief justices of the Supreme Court. Oliver Ellsworth was the second chief justice, serving in the post for nearly five years.*

Letter of a Landholder
November 19, 1787

In the state this country was left by the war, with want of experience in sovereignty, and the feelings which the people then had; nothing but the scene we had passed thro' could give a general conviction that an internal government of strength is the only means of repressing external violence, and preserving the natural rights of the people against the injustice of their own brethren. Even the common duties of humanity will gradually go out of use, when the constitution and laws of a country do not insure justice from the public and between individuals American experience, in our present deranged state, hath again proved these great truths, which have been verified in every age since men were made and became sufficiently numerous to form into public bodies, A government capable of controling the whole, and bringing its force to a point, is one of the prerequisites for national liberty. We combine in society, with an expectation to have our persons and properties defended against unreasonable exactions either at home or abroad....

The present question is, shall we have such a constitution or not? We allow it to be a creation of power; but power when necessary for our good is as much to be desired as the food we eat or the air we breathe. Some men are mightily afraid of giving power lest it should be improved for oppression; this is doubtless possible, but where is the probability? The same objection may be made against the constitution of every state in the union, and against every possible mode of government; because a power of doing good always implies a power to do evil if the person or party be disposed.

The right of the legislature to ordain laws binding on the people, gives them the power to make bad laws.

The right of a judge to inflict punishment gives him both power and opportunity to oppress the innocent; yet none but crazy men will from thence determine that it is best to have neither a legislature nor judges.

If a power to promote the best interest of the people necessarily implies a power to do evil, we must never expect such a constitution in theory as will not be open in some respects to the objections of carping and jealous men. The new Constitution is perhaps more cautiously guarded than any other in the world and at the same time creates a power which will be able to protect the subject; yet doubtless objections may be raised, and so they may against the constitution of each state in the union....

If, my countrymen, you wait for a constitution which absolutely bars a power of doing evil, you must wait long, and when obtained it will have no power of doing good. I allow you are oppressed, but not from the quarter that jealous and wrongheaded men would insinuate. You are oppressed by the men who, to serve their own purposes would prefer the shadow of government to the reality. You are oppressed for the want of power which can protect commerce, encourage business, and create a ready demand for the production of your farms. You are to become poor; oppression continued will make wise men mad. The landholders and farmers have long borne this oppression, we have been patient and groaned in secret, but can promise for ourselves no longer; unless relieved, madness may excite us to actions we now dread....

James Monroe

1758–1831

Born into a relatively modest Virginian family, at seventeen James Monroe left William and Mary College to join the Third Virginia Regiment as a lieutenant in the Revolution. He saw battle in New York, was wounded in Trenton, New Jersey, then served as aide to General William Alexander (1777–1778). He left military service and returned to Virginia after being denied a command. Monroe next studied law with Thomas Jefferson, following in his mentor's footsteps to become the fifth U.S. president. Monroe distinguished himself as a Founding Father through his geniality, integrity and pragmatism, but also beyond these personal characteristics, through his accomplishments as an administrator and diplomat.

Elected to the Virginia House of Delegates in 1782, he became a delegate to the Second Continental Congress (1783–1786), working on the Articles of Confederation. He led opposition to the Jay-Gardoqui proposals, which would have banned U.S. use of the Mississippi, and devised the Northwest Ordinance's territorial government structure. Although a supporter of central government, he did not favor ratification of the U.S. Constitution, because it gave away too much control to the Senate and authorized direct taxation.

After marriage to Elizabeth Kortright, Monroe took up legal practice, moving to Albemarle County to be close to his mentor Jefferson. Monroe joined James Madison to found the Republican Party (today's Democrats) after election to the Senate in 1790. There he supported states rights and strict constructionism against the prevailing Federalist policies. To mollify his Republican critics, President George Washington appointed Monroe minister to France in 1794, and then recalled him two years later for primarily advocating Republican policy.

This brief episode became one of the most controversial of Monroe's career. These years were among the most unsettled—and unsettling—of the French Revolution, yet Monroe was expected to maintain friendship with the new revolutionary government. Only a few days before he arrived, Robespierre, the most radical leader, had been executed, and as the months passed, the situation in Paris became ever more tumultuous. Monroe's open support of the revolutionaries would infuriate the Federalists back in the United States, and in retrospect he does seem somewhat naive, as exemplified by the account in his autobiography of one of the turning points. On October 5, 1795, there was an attempt led by royalists to overthrow the ruling Convention, but it was totally suppressed by troops loyal to the Convention

OPPOSITE: *A portrait of President James Monroe by artist Charles Bird King. Monroe's first term was known as the "Era of Good Feeling," leading to his almost unanimous reelection in 1820—one elector changed his vote so that George Washington would remain the only unanimously elected president.*

that was governing France. It is a most extraordinary snapshot of history: this genteel Virginian statesman supporting a violent military action led by the man dismissed by some as "the Corsican adventurer"—Napoleon Bonaparte.

In the next phase of his career, Monroe served as governor of Virginia (1799–1802) and was praised for his administrative skills and quick action in quashing a slave revolt, Gabriel's Rebellion (also known as the Gabriel Prosser Revolt). A slavery opponent, he proposed resettling freed slaves in the West, but the idea never caught on. In 1803, President Jefferson appointed his protégé special envoy to work with Robert Livingston in negotiating access to a port on the Spanish-held Mississippi River. By the time Monroe arrived, Napoleon, who had just acquired Louisiana from Spain, was offering to sell it to the United States for $15 million. Such a purchase agreement overreached their authority, but Monroe and Livingston jumped at the opportunity, and the Louisiana Purchase was ratified, adding an enormous area to the fledgling nation.

Monroe continued his diplomacy, with an unsuccessful effort to win Spanish approval for the Louisiana Purchase and then was named minister to Great Britain (1803–1807). With special envoy William Pinkney, he won commercial concessions from the British in 1806, but Jefferson balked at signing the treaty because it did not include a ban on impressment of sailors.

In 1810, having reconciled with James Madison, whom he blamed for failure of the 1806 treaty, Monroe (he had permitted his name to be entered against Madison in the presidential race) once again was elected Virginia's

The Monroe Doctrine
December 2, 1823

It was stated at the commencement of the last session that a great effort was then making in Spain and Portugal to improve the condition of the people of those countries, and that it appeared to be conducted with extraordinary moderation. It need scarcely be remarked that the result has been so far very different from what was then anticipated.... The citizens of the United States cherish sentiments the most friendly in favor of the liberty and happiness of their fellowmen on that side of the Atlantic. In the wars of the European powers in matters relating to themselves we have never taken any part, nor does it comport with our policy so to do. It is only when our rights are invaded or seriously menaced that we resent injuries or make preparation for our defense....

We owe it, therefore, to candor and to the amicable relations existing between the United States and those powers to declare that we should consider any attempt on their part to extend their system to any portion of this hemisphere as dangerous to our peace and safety.... In the war between those new Governments and Spain we declared our neutrality at the time of their recognition, and to this we have adhered, and shall continue to adhere, provided no change shall occur which, in the judgment of the competent authorities of this Government, shall make a corresponding change on the part of the United States indispensable to their security....

ABOVE: *French diplomat Marquis François de Barbe-Marbois, Robert Livingston, and James Monroe sign the Louisiana Purchase in Paris on April 30, 1803. The territory acquired in the purchase roughly doubled the area of the United States.*

governor. As president, Madison, beleaguered by the Federalists, tapped his former opponent for secretary of state. The alliance made possible a declaration of war against Great Britain in the War of 1812. With hopes for a military command again frustrated, Monroe became secretary of war after John Armstrong's resignation over British invasion of the capital. He reorganized the Department of War and continued as acting secretary of state. To obtain the 1814 Treaty of Ghent that ended the War of 1812, Monroe authorized the American negotiators to omit any mention of the issue of impressments. He did finally get the British to limit their armed ships on the Great Lakes, however, with the 1817 Rush-Bagot Treaty.

As the third Democrat-Republican in sixteen years, Monroe's election as president in 1816 marked the end of the Federalist party and its power. Monroe's first term was dubbed the "Era of Good Feelings" and he capitalized on it with a tour of the nation. Nationalism characterized his administration, noted for its potent cabinet (the young John Quincy Adams, William Crawford, John C. Calhoun), except in the area of the nation's infrastructure: Monroe viewed federal financing of domestic projects as unconstitutional.

The Era of Good Feelings came to an abrupt end with the controversy over Missouri statehood. Threatening to veto it if statehood for Missouri was contingent on allowing slavery, Monroe signed the Missouri Compromise in 1820 only after admission of the new slave state to the union was balanced by the admission of slavery-free Maine. Through the Adams-Onis Treaty in 1819, Monroe ensured that Florida went from Spanish to U.S. ownership and the boundaries of the Louisiana Territory were clarified.

It was clear by this time that Monroe was presiding over a country that had moved beyond the founding phase and was becoming a full-fledged member of the international community of nations. Nowhere was this more apparent than when Monroe demonstrated his diplomatic skill in his U.S.-Latin American policy. Following the advice of John Quincy Adams, he refused to join forces with Great Britain when France and Spain made plans to resume colonialism there, instead maintaining a policy of neutrality. The United States, he said, considered the Americas closed to colonization, which if undertaken by European nations would be considered "dangerous to our peace and safety." Even though the British foreclosed any imperialism then, the Monroe Doctrine later became a foundation for U.S.-Latin American policy. Monroe was less successful in achieving an agreement with Great Britain over declaring slave trade as piracy, after the Senate so changed its terms that the British rejected the final agreement.

Badgered by infighting among those hoping to succeed him at the end of his term, Monroe retired to his Virginia estate and stayed out of politics except for leading Virginia's Constitutional Convention in 1830. His death in New York, where his daughter was caring for him, marked the end of the era of revolutionary heroes. Not a great speaker or writer, Monroe left his mark through that rare ability to get along with all sides and reach accord.

John Marshall

1775–1835

OPPOSITE: *A portrait of Chief Justice John Marshall by artist Robert Matthew Sully. Marshall was appointed as the nation's fourth chief justice by President John Adams in 1801 and served in the position for nearly thirty-five years.*

John Marshall, fourth chief justice of the United States Supreme Court, developed the bedrock concept that the courts are the final arbitrators on the constitutionality of the actions of the executive branch of government, and of the laws enacted by Congress. Born in 1755, in Prince William (later Fauquier) County, on what was then the Virginia frontier, Marshall received two years of formal schooling, and was largely educated at home by his father. Marshall's frontier upbringing colored his personality (and even his style of dress): For the rest of his life, his contemporaries often commented on his informal, even rough-hewn ways.

When the Revolution erupted, Marshall served as an officer in the Continental army and struggled through the winter of 1777 to 1778 at Valley Forge, alongside "brave men from every colony united in common cause." This experience helped shape both his commitment to the concept of a unified American nation, and his staunch loyalty to the leadership of George Washington.

As a young Virginia legislator and delegate to the state's convention that ratified the Constitution in 1788, Marshall strongly supported the judiciary articles, which he believed defined the role of the judges as guardians of the Constitution. A leading defender of Washington's policies, and a preeminent member of the Federalist Party in Virginia, he was appointed in 1797 by

RIGHT: *John Marshall was an officer in the Continental army that struggled through the winter of 1777 to 1778 at Valley Forge. The experience helped shape his concept of a unified American nation.*

President John Adams to a diplomatic mission to France. Marshall became a national hero when he refused to compromise American sovereignty amid the intrigues, coercion, and corruption he encountered in negotiations with French foreign minister Talleyrand and his anonymous agents, X.,Y., and Z.

In June 1800, John Adams made Marshall secretary of state. When John Adams and the Federalist Party lost both the presidency and the Congress to Jefferson's Democrat-Republican party in the election of 1800, the Federalists used the weeks before Jefferson's inauguration to create new judges and justices of the peace as well as to expand the circuit court system, appointing Federalists to these positions, in a move to perpetuate Federalist control of the judiciary. The appointment of these "midnight judges" was overshadowed by the drama of the electoral college's deadlock between Thomas Jefferson and Aaron Burr. One month before the end of his term in office, Adams appointed Marshall as chief justice of the Supreme Court, whose members were all Federalist appointees. Marshall continued to serve as secretary of state for the remaining weeks of Adams's term, and in that capacity, was responsible for signing and delivering commissions for new judges appointed by President Adams.

Thwarting the intentions of the outgoing Federalist government, the new Democrat-Republican majority in Congress abolished the jobs to which the new circuit judges had been appointed for life; reduced the Supreme Court sessions to once a year; and postponed the next session until 1803. William Marbury, whose commission to the minor post of justice of the peace had been signed but not delivered by Marshall in the last hours of the Adams administration, petitioned the Supreme Court to issue a writ of mandamus, compelling the new secretary of state, James Madison, a Democrat-Republican, to deliver his commission.

The landmark *Marbury v. Madison* case, decided in 1803, threatened the Supreme Court's power of judicial review, and brought the judiciary into direct conflict with the executive and legislative branches of government. It

PROPERTY PROTECTED a la Françoise.

LEFT: *A British cartoon lampooning Franco-American relations following the XYZ affair. John Marshall was one of the three American commissioners to France who were solicited for bribes in exchange for diplomatic access.*

Chief Justice John Marshall
Ruling on Marbury v. Madison
February 24, 1803

The question, whether an act, repugnant to the constitution can become the law of the land is a question deeply interesting to the United States; but, happily, not of an intricacy proportioned to its interest. It seems only necessary to recognize certain principles, supposed to have been long and well established, to decide it....

This original and supreme will organizes the government, and assigns to different departments their respective powers. It may either stop here, or establish certain limits not to be transcended by those departments. The government of the United States is of the latter description. The powers of the legislature are defined and limited, and that those limits may not be mistaken, or forgotten, the constitution is written..... It is a proposition too plain to be contested, that the constitution controls any legislative act repugnant to it; or, that the legislature may alter the constitution by an ordinary act. Between these alternatives there is no middle ground. The constitution is either a superior paramount law, unchangeable by ordinary means, or it is on a level with ordinary legislative acts, and, like other acts, is alterable when the legislature shall please to alter it....

It is emphatically the province and duty of the judicial department to say what the law is. Those who apply the rule to particular cases, must of necessity expound and interpret that rule. If two laws conflict with each other the courts must decide on the operation of each.

So if a law be in opposition to the constitution; if both the law and the constitution apply to a particular case, so that the court must either decide that case conformably to the law, disregarding the constitution; or conformably to the constitution, disregarding the law; the court must determine which of these conflicting rules governs the case. This is of the very essence of judicial duty.....

The judicial power of the United States is extended to all cases arising under the constitution.

Could it be the intention of those who gave this power to say that in using it the constitution should not be looked into? That a case arising under the constitution should be decided without examining the instrument under which it arises?

This is too extravagant to be maintained.

In some cases, then, the constitution must be looked into by the judges. And if they can open it at all, what part of it are they forbidden to read or to obey?...

[I]t is apparent, that the framers of the constitution contemplated that instrument as a rule for the government of courts, as well as of the legislature.....

Thus, the particular phraseology of the constitution of the United States confirms and strengthens the principle, supposed to be essential to all written constitutions, that a law repugnant to the constitution is void; and that courts, as well as other departments, are bound by that instrument....

initially played itself out in a manner close to farce. Marshall led a Court that heard arguments over whether the commissions he knew he had signed had ever existed. Secretary of State Madison ignored the proceedings, and the majority Democrat-Republican Senate refused to produce its records. The Court had no power to enforce its decision, and in the intensely partisan atmosphere of the day, Madison would probably refuse to obey a decision in

FIRST CAPITOL INAUGURATION · 1829

Marbury's favor. In addition, a Democrat-Republican Congress might impeach Marshall for conflict of interest. Yet, if the Court did not assert its independence as the guardian of the Constitution, above intimidation by the president and Congress, it would be admitting it had no power to rule on the acts of other branches of government.

The Court's decision, shaped by Madison was ingenious. Marshall ruled that Section 13 of the Judiciary Act of 1789, which was passed by a Federalist Congress and which gave the Supreme Court the right to compel lower courts or public officials to perform certain actions, was a violation of the Constitution because nowhere did the Constitution give Congress the right to enlarge the original jurisdiction of the Court. In other words, Marshall ruled against his fellow Federalists, including Marbury. But now Madison could not defy a ruling in his favor, even as the Supreme Court had established its power to rule on the constitutionality of laws passed by Congress. In striking down a law passed by Congress that had expanded the Court's jurisdiction, Marshall, although limiting the Court's own area of jurisdiction, had affirmed the Court's power as the final arbiter.

ABOVE: *Chief Justice John Marshall administered the oath of office for President Andrew Jackson's second term on March 4, 1829. It was the last presidential oath administered by Marshall, who had performed the duty a total of nine times for five different presidents.*

Until this point, the Supreme Court had not fully assumed the strong, independent, stabilizing role many had envisioned it would perform under the Constitution. The executive branch ignored laws it did not approve, and some states threatened to decide for themselves what laws to accept. The Court was becoming subservient to the other branches of government. Under Marshall's leadership, over the next thirty years, the Court, which had previously been held in low esteem, delivered rulings that established its non-partisanship, dignity, and wisdom.

Marshall's rulings consistently restricted state sovereignty in two broad categories: when state laws violated a specific constitutional prohibition or restraint on state power; and when a law was incompatible with federal supremacy. In particular, the doctrine of "nullification," by which states claimed the right to declare federal laws unconstitutional—openly advanced by John Calhoun of South Carolina in 1828—foreshadowed the war between the states, and led Marshall to despair of the country's future during the last years of his tenure. But Marshall's leadership had established the Supreme Court as the interpreter and guardian of the Constitution, and set legal precedents that determined the form of "the more perfect union" envisioned in the Constitution.

BELOW: A typically convoluted political cartoon from 1833, predicting dire consequences for President Andrew Jackson's withdrawal of federal funds from the Bank of the United States. At top center, Chief Justice John Marshall protects the statue Justice from the mob attempting to pull it down.

Engraved for the American Gleaner.

W.S.Leney Sculp.t NY.

George Wythe. Esq.r

Engraved for the American Gleaner.

George Wythe

1726–1806

As a representative of Virginia, George Wythe helped to shape a new nation when he penned his signature on the Declaration of Independence. But perhaps Wythe's greatest contribution to the foundation of the United States was as a professor of law who shaped some of the finest minds America has known.

Wythe [pronounced "with"] was born in Elizabeth County, Virginia, in 1726. The middle child of a wealthy plantation owner, Wythe received much of his early education from his mother, who taught him a wide variety of subjects, including Latin and Greek. Wythe went on to study law, mostly on his own, and was admitted to the bar in 1746. In addition to practicing law, Wythe soon entered politics, winning election to the Virginia House of Burgesses in 1754. There he drafted a strident opposition to the Stamp Act, called the Resolutions of Remonstrance, one of the first formal calls for the tax's repeal.

Wythe's strong inclination toward independence and his intimate knowledge of law made him a brilliant addition to the delegation that represented Virginia at the Continental Congress. Wythe was the last of seven Virginians to sign the Declaration of Independence, yet his signature appears at the top of the delegation. It is said that Wythe was held in such high esteem by his colleagues that the top spot was left available so his signature would appear above the rest.

In addition to his work as a legislator, Wythe was very keen on passing along his broad knowledge of law to a new generation. One of his earliest and best students was a young man named Thomas Jefferson. Wythe guided Jefferson through a range of studies, including Roman and Saxon law, encouraging his pupil to study the texts in their original languages, rather than translations. Supreme Court Justice Lewis F. Powell, Jr., said that "through his influence on Jefferson, one could say that Wythe was the godfather of the Declaration of Independence."

In 1779, Jefferson, then Governor of Virginia, appointed Wythe as a professor of law at the College of William and Mary. It was the first law chair ever at an American institution of higher learning. In that position, Wythe had an enormous influence shaping the minds

Legal Argument for the Doctrine of Judicial Review
1782

I have heard of an English chancellor who said, and it was nobly said, that it was his duty to protect the rights of the subject against the encroachments of the crown; and that he would do it, at every hazard. But if it was his duty to protect a solitary individual against the rapacity of the sovereign, surely it is equally mine to protect one branch of the legislature...against the usurpations of the other.... Whenever traitors shall be fairly convicted, by the verdict of their peers before the competent tribunal; if one branch of the legislature, without the concurrence of the other, shall attempt to rescue the offenders from the sentence of the law, I shall not hesitate, sitting in this place, to say to the general court, *Fiat justitia, ruat coelum*; and, to the usurping branch of the legislature, "You attempt worse than a vain thing; for, although you cannot succeed, you set an example which may convulse society to its centre." Nay more, if the whole legislature, an event to be depreciated, should attempt to overleap the bounds prescribed to them by the people, I, in administering the public justice of the country, will meet the united powers at my seat in this tribunal; and, pointing to the constitution, will say to them, "Here is the limit of your authority; and hither shall you go, but no further."...

of future presidents, senators, and Supreme Court justices. Some of his students included James Monroe, John Marshall, and Henry Clay. In 1782, in fact, in one of his most famous legal arguments, even before the United States had adopted its Constitution, Wythe virtually anticipated Marshall's famous ruling that the courts had the final say on the constitutionality of legislation.

Wythe met an untimely death in 1806 when he was allegedly poisoned by his grandnephew, George Wythe Sweeney, who was said to have sought the expeditious death of his great uncle in order to collect an inheritance. The only witness to the crime was one of Wythe's former slaves. Since the law prohibited blacks from testifying in court against whites, Sweeney was acquitted for lack of evidence. Of his former mentor and friend, Thomas Jefferson wrote, "No man ever left behind him a character more venerated than George Wythe. His virtue was of the purest kind; his integrity inflexible and his justice exact. He might truly be called the Cato of his country."

BELOW: *An engraving of the College of William and Mary in Williamsburg, Virginia, circa 1740, where George Wythe was appointed as chair of the law school by Governor Thomas Jefferson in 1779. Wythe had been a teacher and mentor to Jefferson and would also teach John Marshall among other notables.*

Index

Picture Credits

Many of the illustrations in this book were provided by the Library of Congress. The publisher would like to thank the Library of Congress and the following agencies whose pictures appear on the pages noted:

The Granger Collection (New York): pages 1, 2, 20 (top), 41, 47 (top), 53, 62, 84, 96, 97, 101 (bottom), 115, 121, 122, 123, 133, 145, 147, 161, 181, 190

Virginia Historical Society (Richmond, Virginia): pages 71, 188

The Historical Society of Delaware: page 82

United States Mint: page 85

The University of Pennsylvania Archives: page 124